Internet of Things with Intel Galileo

Employ the Intel Galileo board to design a world of smarter technology for your home

Miguel de Sousa

BIRMINGHAM - MUMBAI

Internet of Things with Intel Galileo

First published: July 2015

Production reference: 1240715

Published by Packt Publishing Ltd.
Livery Place
35 Livery Street
Birmingham B3 2PB, UK.

ISBN 978-1-78217-458-5

www.packtpub.com

Credits

Author
Miguel de Sousa

Reviewers
Marcel Meijer
Carlos Montesinos
Gerardo Fco. Carmona Ruiz
Mudit Uppal

Commissioning Editor
Ashwin Nair

Acquisition Editor
Shaon Basu

Content Development Editor
Merwyn D'souza

Technical Editors
Bhupesh Kothari
Rahul C. Shah

Copy Editor
Swati Priya

Project Coordinator
Neha Bhatnagar

Proofreader
Safis Editing

Indexer
Monica Ajmera Mehta

Production Coordinator
Arvindkumar Gupta

Cover Work
Arvindkumar Gupta

About the Author

Miguel de Sousa is a core engineer and full-stack developer at Muzzley. He holds an MSc in computing and telecommunications engineering from ISCTE-IUL Lisbon University Institute, Portugal. He has worked in backend networking, protocols implementation, and systems integration. As a maker, over the last 2 years, he has been developing several projects using Raspberry Pi, Arduino, and Intel Galileo/Edison boards in the field of Internet of Things.

My thanks go to my girlfriend, Vânia, for all her support; my newborn son, Dinis, who was very very upset with me for having to share my attention with the book writing process; and my father, who was always asking me, "Is it ready yet?" I would also like to thank my colleague, Paulo Adrião (communication designer and maker), in particular, for producing all the book photos and images; Pedro Figueiredo (AI lead developer and philosopher), for all his valuable input and the experiences he shared with me; and Tânia Rocha (a passionate frontend developer), for the input and help to develop the visual interfaces for the demos. Thanks to the Intel UK, Wyliodrin, and Muzzley teams for all the help with equipment, support, and troubleshooting.

About the Reviewers

Marcel Meijer has been an all-round Microsoft architect and Microsoft cloud specialist since 2008. He has helped many companies make the jump to successful Microsoft Cloud/Azure implementations. He has worked at consulting companies in the past for customers in different verticals. He combines an in-depth knowledge of both technique and business to make sure that his clients get the optimal solution to make their business competitive.

He is the chairman of the Software Development Network (SDN), and is also an editor and event organizer. He is a frequent blogger and a regular speaker at community events and conferences in the Netherlands. He has been honored with the Microsoft MVP award for 5 years in a row.

Also, Marcel is very interested in IoT, or as he says, the Internet of Everything. He possesses many devices, and they are all connected in some way. In the years to come, the IoT or connected devices will only grow, so it is now the time to get familiar with this. The possibilities are endless.

Carlos Montesinos is a systems architect expert in Internet of Things and robotics. He is an electrical and computer engineer. He is passionate about technology, user experience, and design. Carlos joined Intel in 2008 and he currently leads the Start-up Initiatives Program at Intel Labs. He focuses on enabling wearable, IoT, and robotics start-ups in Silicon Valley and around the world. Carlos also conducts several workshops on to hardware prototyping and connected product development in San Francisco.

Gerardo Fco. Carmona Ruiz holds a BSc in mechatronics engineering and is pursuing his MSc in electronics engineering. He works as a department assistant in the mechatronics and electronics department at the Instituto Tecnologico y de Estudios Superiores de Monterrey in Guadalajara, Mexico. He enjoys teaching science and technology and is passionate about mentoring robotics. In his spare time, he likes woodworking and spending time with his family.

I would like to thank my wife and my son, Santiago, for giving me the space to complete reviewing this book. They have always been supportive.

Mudit Uppal is a multidisciplinary creative technologist and a hacker. He comes has a background in computer science engineering and data visualization, with a keen eye for design and UX. He's currently pursuing his master's at the University of California, where he studies human computer interaction, media arts, and entrepreneurship. He has worked as a creative coder and technologist at companies such as Wieden Kennedy and SapientNitro/Second Story.

He's an avid fan of making new wearable tools using modern micro-controller technologies. He's always looking for interesting projects and people to collaborate with. You can check out his work at `http://www.muppal.com/` or find him on Twitter at `@modqhx`.

I'd like to thank all the people I've worked with in the past, primarily in the domain of wearable computing and IoT devices.

---

www.PacktPub.com

Support files, eBooks, discount offers, and more

For support files and downloads related to your book, please visit www.PacktPub.com.

Did you know that Packt offers eBook versions of every book published, with PDF and ePub files available? You can upgrade to the eBook version at www.PacktPub.com and as a print book customer, you are entitled to a discount on the eBook copy. Get in touch with us at service@packtpub.com for more details.

At www.PacktPub.com, you can also read a collection of free technical articles, sign up for a range of free newsletters and receive exclusive discounts and offers on Packt books and eBooks.

https://www2.packtpub.com/books/subscription/packtlib

Do you need instant solutions to your IT questions? PacktLib is Packt's online digital book library. Here, you can search, access, and read Packt's entire library of books.

Why subscribe?

- Fully searchable across every book published by Packt
- Copy and paste, print, and bookmark content
- On demand and accessible via a web browser

Free access for Packt account holders

If you have an account with Packt at www.PacktPub.com, you can use this to access PacktLib today and view 9 entirely free books. Simply use your login credentials for immediate access.

To my mother, who always encouraged me to face new challenges with a smile, and I did not have the chance to say thank you.

Obrigado, Sãozinha!

Table of Contents

Preface

As technology is evolving, things that surround us in our daily lives are starting to have the ability to share data over the Internet. With this evolution, it is no longer the case that only humans can operate the devices connected to the Internet. These devices are now able to collect and share sensorial data that can be controlled by sensor inputs. They also help you power up big data analysis, monitor systems, and even make devices work together for a common purpose. A new era has begun, the era of Internet of Things!

Following this vision, Intel presented the Galileo board, a board that packs together many of the most common components that are usually purchased separately for most development boards. An Intel Galileo Board can be programmed to read and control sensors and actuators, being an interesting tool for sensorial data collection. The possibility of connecting it straight to the Internet using an Ethernet cable or a wireless card in its mini PCI-express slot enables it to share the collected data over the Internet. Another great feature is that being hardware and software compatible with Arduino, it will make you have a very familiar development environment. If you prefer using other development tools, you can also do that by booting your board from a custom Linux image.

This book will give you the right tools to help you start developing your own IoT projects using an Intel Galileo board.

What this book covers

Chapter 1, *Introducing Galileo*, introduces you to the Intel Galileo boards by explaining their components, main differences when compared to other boards, and the other interesting boards for building IoT projects.

Chapter 2, *Rediscovering the Arduino IDE*, will guide you through the Arduino IDE from the process of setting up your board to uploading and running your first sketches.

Chapter 3, Monitoring the Board Temperature, will help you develop your first IoT project with the Arduino IDE. You'll create and collect temperature data samples from your own board CPU temperature and plot it to an online chart using Galileo as a web client.

Chapter 4, Creating a Motion Sensing Light, will show you how to create a web server with the Arduino IDE and use it to display a web page, allowing you to switch the lighting system operation mode, which is controlled by motion sensor, either by luminosity or manually.

Chapter 5, Intel IoT Developer Kit Tools, introduces you to the Intel ecosystem, giving you an overview of its perks and how you can use its main libraries to read and control your sensors and actuators in other development languages.

Chapter 6, Building an Irrigation System, will guide you through the process of monitoring your sensor data using Wyliodrin, and the creation of rules to control actuators.

Chapter 7, Creating Christmas Light Effects, will teach you how to create remotely controlled animations using an LED strip and a YouTube player.

Chapter 8, The Intel XDK IoT Edition, will explain how you can use the Intel XDK IoT Edition IDE to develop Node.js projects for Galileo.

Chapter 9, Developing an IoT Quiz, will help you develop a quiz game played with mobile devices.

Chapter 10, Integrating with Muzzley, will show you how you can integrate Galileo in your daily life. You'll be creating a building door unlocking system using your Galileo board and integrating it with market-available smart devices using the Muzzley cloud-based ecosystem.

What you need for this book

- An Intel Galileo board (Gen 1 or Gen 2) with the corresponding power supply
- A USB to micro-B cable
- An ethernet cable
- An 8 GB microSD card with adaptor
- Grove Starter Kit Plus sensors kit (Gen 1 or Gen 2)
- A breadboard and jumper wires
- 1k and 10k Ohm resistors
- An LED (5 V max)

- A moisture sensor

- A photocell

- A passive infrared presence sensor

- An HC-SR04 ultrasound sensor

- A digitally addressable LPD8806 LED strip

- A lightbulb with a socket and power plug

- A 220V AC solid state relay, 5 V DC controlled

- An inter communicator with a door unlocker button

- A PC/laptop running Windows, Linux, or Mac OS X with an internal or external SD card reader

All the software you'll be using in this book is available for free.

Who this book is for

This book is intended for developers, hobbyists, and enthusiasts in general. Basic background knowledge of computing, electronics, and microcontroller development with technology such as Arduino or Raspberry Pi boards will make the learning process easier. Also, an awareness of the basic development concepts of Arduino and Node.js (JavaScript) will be helpful.

Conventions

In this book, you will find a number of text styles that distinguish between different kinds of information. Here are some examples of these styles and an explanation of their meaning.

Code words in text, folder names, filenames, file extensions, pathnames, dummy URLs, user input, and Twitter handles are shown as follows: "In the demos you tested in the previous steps, you've tried only the digitalWrite and analogWrite methods."

A block of code is set as follows:

```
socket.on('error', function (error) {
  console.log('Something went wrong!');
});
```

When we wish to draw your attention to a particular part of a code block, the relevant lines or items are set in bold:

```
exports = module.exports = {};
exports.start = runAnimation;
exports.stop = stopAnimation;
```

Any command-line input or output is written as follows:

```
npm install async
```

New terms and **important words** are shown in bold. Words that you see on the screen, for example, in menus or dialog boxes, appear in the text like this: " To see all the available libraries, navigate to **Sketch | Import Library...** on the IDE top menu."

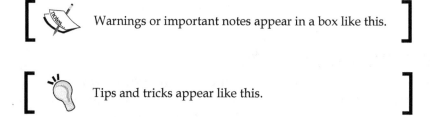

> Warnings or important notes appear in a box like this.

> Tips and tricks appear like this.

Reader feedback

Feedback from our readers is always welcome. Let us know what you think about this book—what you liked or disliked. Reader feedback is important for us as it helps us develop titles that you will really get the most out of.

To send us general feedback, simply e-mail feedback@packtpub.com, and mention the book's title in the subject of your message.

If there is a topic that you have expertise in and you are interested in either writing or contributing to a book, see our author guide at www.packtpub.com/authors.

Customer support

Now that you are the proud owner of a Packt book, we have a number of things to help you to get the most from your purchase.

Downloading the example code

You can download the example code files from your account at `http://www.packtpub.com` for all the Packt Publishing books you have purchased. If you purchased this book elsewhere, you can visit `http://www.packtpub.com/support` and register to have the files e-mailed directly to you.

Downloading the color images of this book

We also provide you with a PDF file that has color images of the screenshots/diagrams used in this book. The color images will help you better understand the changes in the output. You can download this file from `https://www.packtpub.com/sites/default/files/downloads/Internet_of_Things_with_Intel_Galileo_ColoredImages.pdf`.

Errata

Although we have taken every care to ensure the accuracy of our content, mistakes do happen. If you find a mistake in one of our books — maybe a mistake in the text or the code — we would be grateful if you could report this to us. By doing so, you can save other readers from frustration and help us improve subsequent versions of this book. If you find any errata, please report them by visiting `http://www.packtpub.com/submit-errata`, selecting your book, clicking on the **Errata Submission Form** link, and entering the details of your errata. Once your errata are verified, your submission will be accepted and the errata will be uploaded to our website or added to any list of existing errata under the Errata section of that title.

To view the previously submitted errata, go to `https://www.packtpub.com/books/content/support` and enter the name of the book in the search field. The required information will appear under the **Errata** section.

Piracy

Piracy of copyrighted material on the Internet is an ongoing problem across all media. At Packt, we take the protection of our copyright and licenses very seriously. If you come across any illegal copies of our works in any form on the Internet, please provide us with the location address or website name immediately so that we can pursue a remedy.

Please contact us at copyright@packtpub.com with a link to the suspected pirated material.

We appreciate your help in protecting our authors and our ability to bring you valuable content.

Questions

If you have a problem with any aspect of this book, you can contact us at questions@packtpub.com, and we will do our best to address the problem.

1
Introducing Galileo

The **Internet of Things (IoT)** is a hot topic nowadays. It is a vision where everyday objects are connected, and share data over the Internet. It is believed that it will have a huge impact in our lives by changing the way we interact with the things that are present in our daily lives.

In this context, many development boards have been developed for the makers' community over the last few years. Most of them required some of the essential components to be bought separately, such as the Ethernet socket. Intel offered a different solution packing the most common components together onboard and putting the Arduino and Linux worlds together, all in one board—the Galileo.

In this chapter, you will be able to understand what the concept of the Internet of Things is, what a Thing is, and how Galileo may help you develop your Things.

In this chapter, we'll be covering the following topics:

- The Internet of Things vision
- Galileo board and its components
- Galileo Gen 2
- Popular boards comparison

The Internet of Things vision

The Internet of Things concept is neither entirely new nor is a futuristic distant technology. It is being built today with today's technology, and you can find it in some of your own home devices, big data clouds, and sensors. It started with wireless technologies converging progressively with **micro-electromechanical systems (MEMS)** and the Internet.

The initial concept suggested that it were the persons who should share the data. Today, it can be defined as a network of sensing and actuating devices with the ability to share information.

The first time the term "Internet of Things" was officially used in a publication back in 1999, where Kevin Ashton published his vision in the *RFID Journal*:

> *You can't eat bits, burn them to stay warm or put them in your gas tank. Ideas and information are important, but things matter much more. Yet today's information technology is so dependent on data originated by people that our computers know more about ideas than things. If we had computers that knew everything there was to know about things – using data they gathered without any help from us – we would be able to track and count everything, and greatly reduce waste, loss and cost. We would know when things needed replacing, repairing or recalling, and whether they were fresh or past their best. The Internet of Things has the potential to change the world, just as the Internet did. Maybe even more so.*

As you can see, devices sharing data is the real concept behind IoT. Such devices could either be living or inanimate. A Thing in the IoT context can be a person wearing a pulse monitor, a dog carrying a tracking device, a garbage bin that notifies it needs to be emptied, or a thermostat that adjust itself automatically to help you lower your electricity bills.

IoT assumes that Things must be uniquely identifiable and able to gather data recurring to sensors. They must also have the ability to communicate and transfer data over a network. Such data could be used for monitoring purposes, big data processing, or even to control that same Thing.

Things supporting this machine-to-machine communication are usually known as smart devices. An example of a smart device is the famous Google Nest thermostat (`https://nest.com/thermostat`). Being more than a simple thermostat, it shares its usage data to help you save on your home's energy, while keeping you cozy. It can also work together with other smart devices such as some Mercedes-Benz cars (`https://nest.com/works-with-nest/`). The car GPS system shares data with the Nest cloud, making it possible to start heating or cooling your home, based on the expected arrival time.

Introducing Intel Galileo

Intel® Galileo is a development board based on Intel x86 architecture; it was designed mostly for makers and complies with open source software and hardware licenses. If you are familiar with the Arduino boards, you'll find this board somewhat similar; the reason being this board was designed to be hardware and software compatible with the Arduino shield ecosystem. It combines Intel technology with support for Arduino shields and libraries. It is even possible to write code using the same Arduino development environment.

The expansion header is similar to the Arduino ones. It has 14 digital I/O pins (where six of them can be used as PWM), six analog inputs, a serial port, and an ICSP header. It supports shields operating at either 3.3 V or 5 V. A jumper on the board enables voltage translation at the I/O pins from 5 V to 3.3 V, and vice versa, providing compatibility with the Arduino shields.

Galileo runs over a very light open source Linux OS in its 8 MB flash memory. However, do take into consideration that Arduino is being emulated using Linux, and your code will be running in a separate process.

This board includes a 10/100 Ethernet connector port, and if you wish to use Wi-Fi, you can add a card to the Mini PCIe socket on the back side of the board.

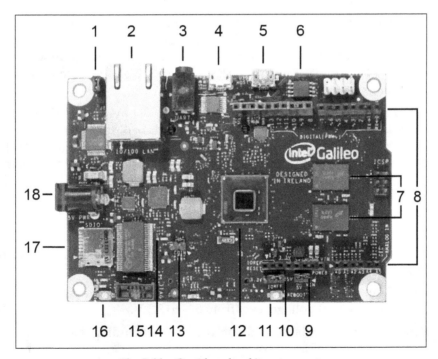

The Galileo Gen 1 board and its components

Breaking down the board, you can find the following major components:

1. **I2C jumper**: This jumper allows you to change the I2C address of some on-board components. You may need to do this if you are using I2C components that conflict with other components on the board.

2. **Ethernet port**: This port allows you to connect your board to a wired network, allowing you to communicate with other devices and also access the Internet. If you wish to use Wi-Fi, in the backside of the board, you'll find a Mini PCI Express slot where you can connect your Wi-Fi card. It also enables another possible storage device, USB host, bluetooth, or GSM card.

3. **Serial port**: There is a serial port for connecting to the Galileo Linux command line from your computer. Although this port looks like an audio jack, it is only used for serial communication.

4. **USB client**: When developing with the Arduino IDE, you'll need to connect your USB cable here, so that you can upload your project's code on the board.

5. **USB host**: Do not mistake this port for the USB client. This one is not intended to be used to upload your project's code, but to allow you to connect more peripheral devices, such as webcams and extra storage.

6. **Flash memory**: This type of memory is persistent and it is where the board firmware is stored, taking most of the available 8 MB of space.

7. **Random Access Memory (RAM)**: This is where your sketches are stored while running. Galileo has 512 KB of in-built SRAM and an additional 256 MB of external DRAM. Since it is a volatile type of memory, when you reboot your board, your sketch will be lost. If you wish to keep it persistent, you'll need to save it to a microSD card.

8. **Arduino expansion header**: It has 14 digital I/O pins (IO2-IO13, TX, RX); all of them can be used as input or output and six of them can be used as **Pulse Width Modulation (PWM)** outputs. The RX and TX pins control the programmable speed UART port. At the bottom-right side of the expansion header, you'll find six available analog pins with a 12-bit resolution. The pins at the bottom -left of the board are power pins (IOREF, VIN, RESET, 3.3 V, 5 V, and 2 GND).

9. **VIN jumper**: This jumper connects the Galileo VIN pin to the 5 V regulator. When using shields that require more voltage than this, you must pull out this jumper to avoid damaging the board.

10. **IOREF jumper**: In order to support 3.3 V shields, you can use this jumper to change your board voltage level from 5 V to 3.3 V.

11. **Reboot button**: This button reboots the board, including the OS.

12. **Intel Quark SoC X1000 Application Processor**: This is the board's processor; it is responsible for processing your code. It is a 32-bit, single core, single-thread, Pentium (P54C/i586) **instruction set architecture (ISA)**-compatible CPU. It is capable of operating at speeds up to 400 MHz.

13. **Clock battery power**: With this inclusion, you won't need to get the date and time from the Internet every time you reboot your board. By connecting a 3 V coin cell battery to the board, you'll be able to keep track of time, even when the board is powered off.

14. **On board LED**: This is an on-board LED, directly connected to the pin 13. You can use it to test and run basic sketches.

15. **JTAG header**: This is used to debug boards. It should be used with an in-circuit debugger.

16. **Reset button**: Pressing this button will restart your code and send the reset signal to the connected shields. It won't restart the OS.

17. **MicroSD card slot**: You'll definitely need more space to store your sketches or other apps. Here, you can insert your microSD card and store your persistent sketches or even use it to boot an operating system instead of the on-board one. You'll need to do this if you want additional functionalities, such as Wi-Fi, since those drivers can't fit in the 8 MB of the board's flash memory. It can be done using a card up to 32 GB.

18. **Power input**: This is where you must connect your power adapter. The 5 V, 2A feed is the only official way to power the board. Intel recommends you power the board through its power supply before connecting it via USB to your computer, otherwise, you might damage your board.

As you can see, this board is more suitable to work with sensors. The Arduino shield compatibility, familiar IDE, real-time clock and, possibility of using the PCI express connector are some of its best features.

Galileo Gen 2

Many makers found the 400 MHz processor a bit slow for their projects, mostly because of Arduino being emulated with Linux. Intel addressed the community issues, made some changes to the original board, and presented a new one named Galileo Gen 2.

Galileo Gen 2 is still powered by the same processor, but its performance has been considerably increased. The Arduino shields compatibility has also been improved with 12 GPIOs, now made fully native by being connected directly to the Quark X1000 SoC, and 12-bit PWM resolution allowing faster and smoother responses.

This board is a bit bigger than the original one, and the 3.5 mm serial port jack has been replaced by a six-pin 3.3 V USB TTL UART header, now making it compatible with the standard FTDI to USB serial cable. Also, the USB host port was replaced with a full size Type A receptacle 2.0 USB port.

The power regulation system has been changed to accept power supplies from 7 V to 15 V. The power supply jack isn't the only powering option available; it is now possible to power this board through the Ethernet cable by connecting it to a **Power over Ethernet (PoE)**-enabled Ethernet switch. It is also possible to power it from a connected shield, as long as the input voltage applied to the Galileo's VIN pin is in the 7 V – 15 V range:

Intel Galileo Gen 2 board

For the demos in this book, you can either use Galileo or Galileo Gen 2. The projects will run on both.

A comparison of Galileo with the most popular boards

Along with Galileo, Raspberry Pi and Arduino Yún are very popular boards among makers. All of them are Linux-embedded and have open source hardware design.

The following is a table with some features of each board:

Features	Intel Galileo	Arduino Yún	Raspberry Pi model B
CPU speed	400 Mhz	400 Mhz	700 Mhz
Memory	256 MB	64 MB (AR9331) and 2.5 KB (ATmega)	512 MB
Internal storage	8 MB	16 MB (AR9331) and 32 KB (ATmega)	-
External storage	MicroSD	MicroSD	SD card
Networking	Ethernet and Wi-Fi (Wi-Fi adapter is bought separately)	Ethernet and Wi-Fi	Ethernet and Wi-Fi (Wi-Fi dongle is bought separately)
Video output	-	-	HDMI and 1080p composite RCA
Audio output	-	-	HDMI and 3.5 mm audio jack
Digital I/O pins	14 at 3.3 V or 5 V	20 at 5 V	17 at 3.3 V
Analog input	6 (12-bit ADC)	12 (10-bit ADC)	-
PWM output	6	7	1
Real-time clock	Optional	-	-
SPI	1	1	2
I2C	1	1	1

Here's the brief comparison of the boards:

- **Arduino Yún**: At first glance, we can say that Yún and Galileo have more in common than with the Raspberry Pi. The number of available PWM, analog and digital pins make them good boards for projects with sensors. Arduino Yún is compatible with most Arduino Leonardo shields. Although Galileo shares a look alike development environment and board setup, not all the shields are compatible because some of the Arduino libraries are heavily bound to the Arduino architecture. Galileo runs a custom Yocto-based Linux in its 8 MB SPI flash by default. To be able to install stronger tools, it requires to be booted from a microSD card image provided by Intel. Yún runs an OpenWrt distribution, and has 16 MB of space available for the entire operating system. It is not possible to boot load from the microSD card, but is possible to increase its disk space by plugging in a microSD card and configuring it to become the new Linux file system. An advantage of Yún is that it already brings Wi-Fi on its board. Galileo requires connecting a Wi-Fi adapter.

- **Raspberry Pi**: Raspberry Pi, the board with the biggest community, is the only board in our table that has video and audio output, making it more interesting for multimedia projects. However, the lack of analog inputs makes this board less interesting to work with analog sensors.

Galileo is compatible with Arduino in the way that it can run 3.3 and 5 V shields, but it has some restrictions because of the Arduino's AVR libraries dependencies. Before buying a shield, you should check whether it is supported by Galileo.

Some of the advantages of the Galileo board when compared to the mentioned ones are the possibilities of working with PCI Express mini cards and using a real-time clock. Besides these, Galileo comes fully ready to work with sensors; this makes it an interesting tool for data collection.

Like the Raspberry Pi, the possibility of booting from a stronger Linux image makes it possible for projects developed in some of the most popular languages such as Python or Node.js (Javascript).

Summary

Galileo is a good option if you have a project requiring sensors, monitoring, or device control. It is an interesting board to develop ambitious projects in the scope of the Internet of Things, where you can develop your unique Things and make them share data with each other.

In this chapter, you've learned about the IoT concept, your board components, and where you should connect what. By now, you may already be able to imagine what you are able to use and connect to your board.

In the next chapter, you'll get familiar with the Arduino development environment, learning how you can develop code and run it in your Galileo.

2
Rediscovering the Arduino IDE

In the previous chapter you learned about the Galileo components and its resemblances to the Arduino development boards, mostly at the hardware level. In this chapter, we'll approach the software level by exploring the Arduino **Integrated Development Environment** (**IDE**) and learning how to use it to develop simple projects.

In this chapter, you'll learn about:

- Setting up your board
- Using the Galileo Arduino IDE
- Updating the Galileo firmware
- Compiling, uploading, and running simple sketches
- Using basic Arduino output methods

Setting up your board

To be able to use this software, you must first connect your board to a computer so that you can exchange data with it. You'll need at least a computer, a power supply, and a USB A to Micro USB Type B cable. The computer that will be used to run the Arduino IDE must be connected to your board.

The power supply comes already with your Galileo, but the USB cable doesn't and you will need to get one separately.

The following diagrams will show you how to wire your Galileo and Galileo Gen 2 boards. The first thing to do should be connecting the power supply and keeping the USB cable ready and unplugged.

[To prevent damaging your board, be sure that whenever you power up your Galileo your USB cable is disconnected from the board.]

As soon as you connect it, you can plug in the USB cable.

[Beware that in the Galileo Gen 1 board, you'll find two USB ports, one tagged as host and the other as client. You must plug in your cable to the client one.]

In the following figures you can also see the Ethernet cable plugged in, but at this stage it is optional:

Wiring up Intel Galileo

The following image is for Galileo Gen 2:

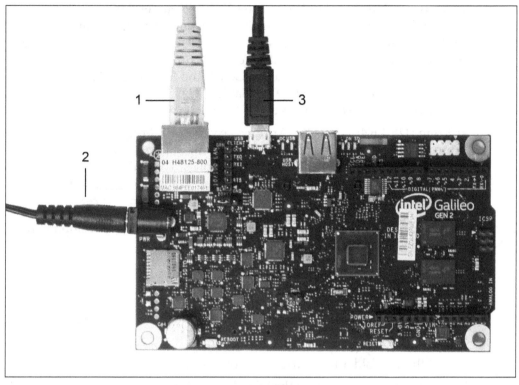

Wiring up the Intel Galileo Gen 2

Downloading and installing the IDE

Having the board ready, let's now install the Arduino IDE on your computer. Currently, there are three main versions of the Arduino IDE—one maintained by Intel (Arduino 1.6.0 – Intel 1.04), another by Arduino.cc (Arduino LLC 1.6.4), and the third one by Arduino.org (Arduino Srl 1.7.3)—appearing after a dispute with Arduino.cc. All of these versions are forks of the same project, but currently only Intel and Arduino.cc IDE's most recent versions support the Intel Galileo boards. Besides having different version numbers, these IDEs are maintained by different entities, and a higher version from a different entity doesn't necessarily mean a more recent version.

You can choose from one of the following versions, which support Intel Galileo:

- **Intel custom Arduino IDE 1.6.0 – Intel 1.04 (recommended)**: This is the Intel Arduino IDE version supporting their boards out of the box, without the need to install any support extensions. It is a custom Arduino IDE with the same functionalities as the original one, but it supports Intel development boards such as Galileo Gen 1, Galileo Gen 2, and Edison. It is the recommended version to work with Galileo. You can download this version at `https://communities.intel.com/community/makers/drivers`.

- **Arduino IDE 1.6.4**: This is the Arduino.cc version. It brings some improvements such as the possibility of adding support to a great range of development boards, including the Intel ones. To be able to use the Intel boards with this IDE, you'll need to install an extension. You can download this version from `http://www.arduino.cc/en/Main/Software`.

Feel free to download the version you prefer since the code we'll be developing in this book will run well on both.

After the selected download completes, extract the downloaded compressed file contents:

For Microsoft Windows 7/8 OS, you need to perform the following steps:

1. You can use 7-Zip (`http://www.7-zip.org/`) to extract the file contents. Extract the `IDE` folder to the root directory of `C:`.

2. The next thing to do is install the USB drivers. If you downloaded the Intel IDE version, the drivers come included and should be located at the `C:\arduino-1.6.0+Intel/drivers` folder. If you downloaded the Arduino.cc IDE, you'll need to download the drivers available at `http://downloadmirror.intel.com/24748/eng/IntelGalileoFirmwareUpdater-1.0.4-Windows.zip` and extract its contents. This download includes the USB drivers and the firmware updater tool.

3. To install the drivers, you must first connect the Galileo to your computer. Windows will try to install the drivers from online sources, but it will fail. Open **Device Manager** from the Windows **Control Panel**, and under the **Ports (COM & LPT)** tab, you'll find your Galileo with the name Gadget Serial:

Windows device manager without the USB drivers installed

4. Right click on it and select **Update Driver Software…**. Now, you need to click on **Browse my computer for driver software**. If you downloaded the Intel IDE version, enter the path `C:\arduino-1.6.0+Intel/drivers` and click on **Next**. If you downloaded the Arduino.cc IDE version instead, go to the `Galileo Driver` folder you just downloaded and extracted and click on **Next**.

5. When the drivers are found in the location you provided, you'll be prompted to install them and you should click on **Install**.

   As soon as the drivers finish installing, you'll be able to find Galileo listed under the **Ports (COM & LPT)** section:

6. To start the IDE, double-click on the Arduino icon inside its folder.

> If you need further assistance installing the USB drivers, check the Intel guides at https://software.intel.com/en-us/articles/intel-galileo-board-assembly.

For Linux OS, use the following steps:

1. You can extract the folder using the following xz command (the filename may be different depending on whether you are running a 32-bit or 64-bit Linux):

   ```
   unxz IntelArduino-1.6.0-Linux64.txz
   ```

2. If you don't have xz installed, you can install it with the following command:

   ```
   $ sudo apt-get install xz-utils
   ```

3. If you are running a Debian Linux, Red Hat, Fedora, CentOS, or similar, use the following command:

   ```
   $ sudo yum install xz
   ```

4. To run the IDE, enter the extracted folder and run this command:

   ```
   ./arduino
   ```

For Mac OS X OS, use the following steps:

1. Unzip the application and move it into your Applications folder.

> If you already have any of the Arduino IDEs, you can rename the folder to something more intuitive (for example, galileoIDE), just make sure there are no spaces in the name of the directory.

2. Double-click on your newly downloaded Arduino application to run the IDE.

3. If you installed the Intel Arduino version, when you run it you'll be asked if you want to update to the latest version of the Arduino IDE. You must click on the **No** option or your IDE will be replaced by the Arduino.cc one.

4. If the installed version was the Arduino.cc IDE 1.6.4, you'll need to add the Intel boards' support. To do it, click on the IDE **Tools** top menu and navigate to **Board | Boards Manager...**. In the displayed list, locate and click on the **Intel i586 Boards by Intel** section and finally click on **Install**:

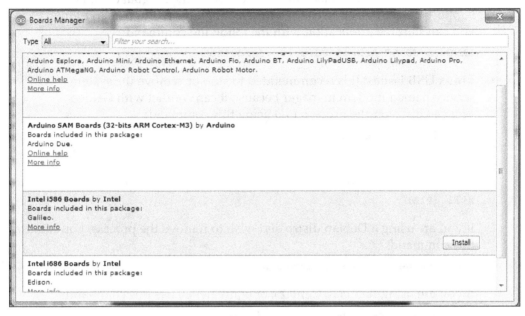

Installing the Intel boards support on Arduino 1.6.4

5. When the installation process completes, you can confirm whether everything went right by navigating to **Tools | Board** in the top menu and finding the Galileo boards listed.

6. When it finishes installing, if everything went right, you should see the **INSTALLED** tag appearing on the selected section.

7. Now, if you navigate to **Tools | Board**, you'll find the Galileo boards appearing in the supported boards list.

Common issues and troubleshooting

The following are some of the commonly faced issues:

- **Unable to access serial port in Linux**: If you aren't able to access the serial port, you may need to run the software with the following command:

```
sudo ./arduino
```

- **Java missing error**: If you get an error related to Java not being found, you must install it using this command:

```
sudo apt-get install default-jre
```

- **Language error**: If you have an error related to the language not being supported, you'll need to change the OS language to English. In Linux, you can start the application with the following command:

```
LANG=en_US LC_ALL=en_US.utf8 ./arduino
```

- **Linux USB issues**: It is recommended to stop or remove the system service named modem manager because it can conflict with Galileo. You can discover the process PID using this command:

```
ps -ef | grep modem*
```

Kill it with the following command, replacing [PID] with the process identification number, visible with the preceding command:

```
kill [PID]
```

If you are using a Debian distro and wish to remove the process, you can use this command:

```
sudo apt-get remove modemmanager
```

If you are using Red Hat, CentOS, or equivalents, use this command:

```
yum remove modemmanager
```

- **Other**: If you are facing a different issue, check the Intel community support forums at https://communities.intel.com/community/tech/galileo/content. If you still can't find any information regarding your issue, open a new question and the Intel support team will help you.

Updating the board firmware

To update your board firmware, you'll need to download the Intel Firmware updater tool. If you are running Windows, you should have this tool already. It comes with the Windows drivers. If you don't have it, or you are running another OS, you can download it at https://software.intel.com/en-us/iot/hardware/galileo/downloads. You can find the right download for your OS listed under the **Intel® Galileo On-board Flash Firmware Updater** section. Download and extract its contents. Execute the firmware-updater-1.0.4.exe file by clicking on it, and the firmware updater interface should be displayed. Ensure you have your Galileo connected to your computer, and in the updater tool, select the USB port you are using. In the same firmware updater tool, check the current and target firmware version. If the current version is lower than the target one, you should update it.

Before updating your board's firmware, ensure that it is properly connected to an external power supply and that there are no SD cards in the SD card reader.

If you need to remove the SD card from the reader, disconnect the USB cable first and then the power cable. Remove the SD card, power the board, and a couple of seconds later, connect the USB cable.

Click on the **Update Firmware** button to start the firmware update process, and you should see this screen:

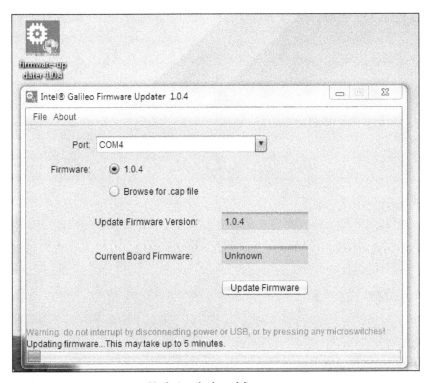

Updating the board firmware

The process should take around five minutes to conclude. During the update process, you can neither power off the board, nor remove the USB cable. Doing this might damage or even brick your board.

Now that we have our board's setup concluded, let's have a look at the Arduino IDE to understand how it works.

The Arduino IDE

The code you write is named `sketch`. With the Arduino IDE, you'll be able to compile your sketches and upload them to your Galileo. Open your Arduino IDE, and you'll find the following environment:

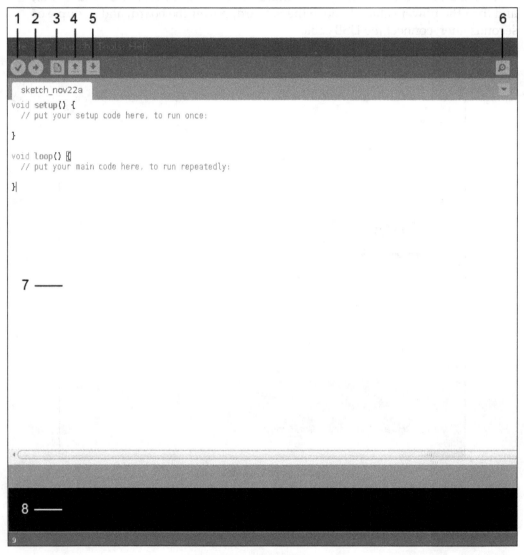

Galileo Arduino IDE

Identifying the IDE components, you can find:

- **Verify**: This button will be your best friend. It will help you compiling your sketch and troubleshooting any issues or syntax errors..

- **Upload**: It will verify your code and, if it has no errors, it will upload your program to the board.

- **New**: It creates a new sketch.

- **Open**: This opens an existing sketch.

- **Save**: It saves your sketch. The saved sketches have the file extension .ino.

- **Serial monitor**: This opens the serial monitor window, which displays serial data from Galileo. This monitor window also allows you to send messages to your board.

- **Your sketch**: This is where you will write your code.

- **Console**: It gives feedback about the operations you are doing. If errors are found when you verify your sketch, they will also be displayed here, usually in red.

Running your first sketches

Now that we have everything set up, let's try to run some simple sketches to make you feel more comfortable with the IDE. Here, you'll be testing how to blink and fade an LED.

In these demos, at least for the fade example, you'll need:

- **A small breadboard**: This type of solderless circuit allows you to build electronic circuits without any soldering while being reusable.

- **An LED**: We'll use a 5 V LED.

- **A resistor**: Depending on the LED type, color, and manufacturer, different resistors will be required. To be able to support a wider range of LEDs, let's use a 1 kΩ resistor. This resistor is represented by the color code brown, black, red, and silver, and it will help you avoid damaging the LED.

Blinking an LED

In this example, you'll be blinking an LED repeatedly over time. This is a very simple demo that is used many times as a test to check whether everything is properly configured and running:

1. Ensure your Galileo is powered up and the USB cable is connected to your computer.

2. Open Arduino IDE you had installed in the previous steps. Locate the **Tools** tab on the top, click on the **Board** option and select the board you'll be using (**Galileo** or **Galileo Gen 2**).

3. Next, you need to select a port for your serial communication. In the same **Tools** menu, click on the **Serial Port** option and select your port:

    º   In Mac OS X, the port starts with `/dev/cu.usbmodem` or `/dev/tty.usbmodem`

    º   In Linux, the port should start with `/dev/ttyACM`

    º   In Windows, it's one of the COM ports

4. Now that you have everything set up, you can open the example `sketch` by navigating to **File | Examples | 1.Basics | Blink**.

You'll now have the Blink sketch in your editor. Now, if you click on the Verify button, you'll be able to see its result in the console. At the end, it will print something like this:

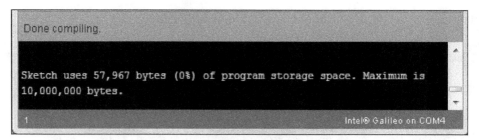

Done compiling.

Sketch uses 57,967 bytes (0%) of program storage space. Maximum is 10,000,000 bytes.

Intel® Galileo on COM4

Verifying a sketch

This means your sketch has no errors, and that it is occupying `57,967 bytes` of the total `10,000,000 bytes` of maximum program storage space available.

Now, by clicking on the Upload button, you'll be able to run the sketch in your board. If everything went fine, you'll see a `Transfer complete` message in the console and an on-board LED blinking every second.

The whole idea behind this demo consists of exporting the pin 13, configuring it as an output, and then keep doing digital writes from high to low inside a loop.

The following code will explain this more clearly:

```
/*
  Blink
  Turns on an LED on for one second, then off for one second,
repeatedly.

  Most Arduinos have an on-board LED you can control. On the Uno and
  Leonardo, it is attached to digital pin 13. If you're unsure what
  pin the on-board LED is connected to on your Arduino model, check
  the documentation at http://arduino.cc

  This example code is in the public domain.

  modified 8 May 2014
  by Scott Fitzgerald
*/
```

The pin 13 was selected because it is directly connected to the on-board LED you can see blinking. If you connect an LED to that I/O, you'll have them both blinking:

```
// the setup function runs once when you press reset or power the
board
void setup() {
  // initialize digital pin 13 as an output.
  pinMode(13, OUTPUT);
}
// the loop function runs over and over again forever
void loop() {
  digitalWrite(13, HIGH);    // turn the LED on (HIGH is the voltage
level)
  delay(1000);               // wait for a second
  digitalWrite(13, LOW);     // turn the LED off by making the voltage
LOW
  delay(1000);               // wait for a second
```

The sketches always have two main functions — the setup and the loop. The setup function will only be called once, and it is commonly used for initial configuration. In this example, you can see the pinMode method being called inside this method, exporting the LED (connected to pin 13) for the application and setting its direction as OUTPUT.

Inside the `loop` method, you'll find that pin 13 is repeatedly being set from `HIGH` to `LOW`, and vice-versa. Those changes are made using the `digitalWrite` method, which is responsible for changing the pin voltage level from 0 V to 5 V and from 5 V to 0 V. The `delay` method helps the LED keep its state every second (1,000 ms) after a state change.

Fading an LED

In this example, you'll be able to understand how to fade an LED. Plug in your resistor, LED, and jumper wires to the breadboard, as shown in the following figure:

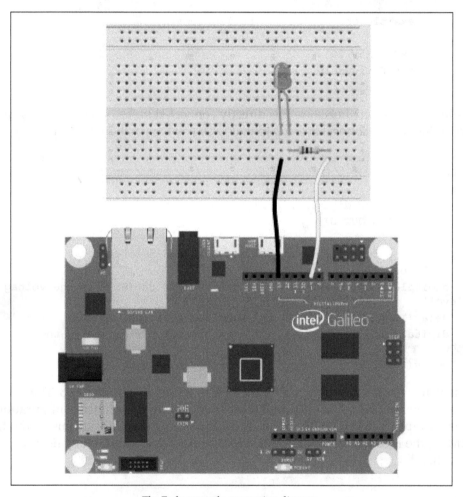

The Fade example connection diagram

Connect one jumper wire from Galileo pin 9 (digital PWM) to one side of the resistor. The other side of the resistor should be connected with the anode of the LED (the longer lead). Finally, the LED cathode (shorter lead) should be connected to the Galileo ground.

Coming back to the IDE, you'll find this example sketch by navigating to **File | Examples | 1.Basics | Fade**. With the example loaded into your sketch, verify and upload it to your board.

As soon as the upload is complete, you should see the LED fading in and out repeatedly over time.

In the previous example, you were able to set two LED states, on and off, using the `digitalWrite` method. In order to have more states, we will need to use the `analogWrite` method. The LED seems to have more than two states. This happens because `analogWrite` uses a property named **pulse with modulation (PWM)**. It accepts values from the range of 0 up to 255:

```
Looking at the code, we have:/*
  Fade

  This example shows how to fade an LED on pin 9
  using the analogWrite() function.

  This example code is in the public domain.
  */
int led = 9;             // the pin that the LED is attached to
Only pins with PWM are supported, Galileo has available the pins 3, 5,
6, 9, 10 and 11.
int brightness = 0;      // how bright the LED is
int fadeAmount = 5;      // how many points to fade the LED by

// the setup routine runs once when you press reset:
void setup()  {
  // declare pin 9 to be an output:
  pinMode(led, OUTPUT);
}
```

Every `loop` cycle, the amount of brightness is increased by 5 units until it reaches the PWM maximum of 255 or decreased by 5 units until it reaches 0:

```
// the loop routine runs over and over again forever:
void loop()  {
  // set the brightness of pin 9:
```

```
    analogWrite(led, brightness);

    // change the brightness for next time through the loop:
    brightness = brightness + fadeAmount;

    // reverse the direction of the fading at the ends of the fade:
    if (brightness == 0 || brightness == 255) {
      fadeAmount = -fadeAmount ;
    }
    // wait for 30 milliseconds to see the dimming effect
    delay(30);
}
```

Using the serial port for debugging

Sometimes, you need to have a bit more feedback about the operations you are doing, display some variables values, or just output something so that you can see your code flow. In such situations, printing to the Galileo serial port can be very helpful.

Using the fade LED demo, we can add some outputs so that we can understand what's happening.

The `Serial.begin(baud_rate)` method opens the Galileo serial port and sets its speed to the specified baud rate. You can then start writing using the `Serial.print()` and `Serial.println()` methods if you wish to change line at the end of the writing.

In your previous code, you can add the following lines:

```
/*
Fade

 This example shows how to fade an LED on pin 9
 using the analogWrite() function.

 This example code is in the public domain.
 */

int led = 9;            // the pin that the LED is attached to
int brightness = 0;     // how bright the LED is
int fadeAmount = 5;     // how many points to fade the LED by

// the setup routine runs once when you press reset:
void setup()  {
```

Initialize the serial port and set up the data transfer baud rate to 9600:

```
Serial.begin(9600);
// declare pin 9 to be an output:
pinMode(led, OUTPUT);
```

Print a line with a custom message to confirm that it is working:

```
Serial.println("Setup is concluded!");
}
```

```
// the loop routine runs over and over again forever:
void loop()  {
```

Print the text keeping the "cursor" in the same line:

```
Serial.print("Brightness value is ");
```

Print the brightness value and move the "cursor" to the next line:

```
Serial.println(brightness);
// set the brightness of pin 9:
analogWrite(led, brightness);

// change the brightness for next time through the loop:
brightness = brightness + fadeAmount;

// reverse the direction of the fading at the ends of the fade:
if (brightness == 0 || brightness == 255) {
  fadeAmount = -fadeAmount ;
}
// wait for 30 milliseconds to see the dimming effect
delay(30);
```

Downloading the example code

You can download the example code files from your account at
http://www.packtpub.com for all the Packt Publishing books
you have purchased. If you purchased this book elsewhere, you
can visit http://www.packtpub.com/support and register to
have the files e-mailed directly to you.

Verify and upload this code on your board. As soon as it is uploaded, click on the Serial monitor button, the one with a magnifying glass in the top right corner. In the serial Monitor window, select the **9600 baud** rate, matching the same baud rate specified in the sketch. You should now be able to see the brightness values being displayed, as shown in the following screenshot:

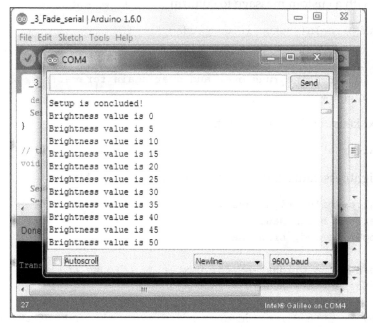

The serial output

Methods and libraries

In the demos you tested in the previous steps, you've tried only the digitalWrite and analogWrite methods. Besides those, there are also the analog methods. On the Arduino website, you can find a useful Arduino language reference explaining all the supported methods, constants, operators, and syntax. You can find the Arduino language reference at http://arduino.cc/en/Reference/HomePage.

The Galileo Arduino IDE already brings some libraries, and it is even possible to import the libraries developed by the Galileo community. Beware, not all the Arduino libraries currently work in Galileo. Many of them were developed strictly for the Arduino architecture, and they require to be ported.

Some of the many libraries that Intel have made available are:

- **Ethernet**: This library allows you to connect to the Internet.
- **WiFi**: This allows you to connect to the Internet using a wireless card. It brings sketches that help you to configure your Wi-Fi access.
- **Wire**: This allows you to communicate with I2C devices.
- **SPI**: This helps you to write to the SPI bus.
- **Servo**: This helps you to control servos smoothly.

 To see all the available libraries, navigate to **Sketch | Import Library...** on the IDE top menu.

Summary

Being part Intel's compatibility with the Arduino world, the Arduino IDE is a very simple and easy-to-use development tool. It allows developers to develop applications for Galileo, Arduino, and many other boards.

This chapter refers to the first steps of setting up your board, installing a suitable Arduino IDE supporting Galileo boards, and running some example sketches. By now, you should already have your IDE installed and ready for the next projects, having some basic notions on how to use it.

In the next chapter, you will use it to read the Galileo's CPU temperature and plot it over time. You'll also learn how to use Galileo as a web client.

3

Monitoring the Board Temperature

As you saw in the previous chapter, Arduino Galileo IDE is very simple to use and by now, you should already know how to compile and upload your sketches to the board.

One interesting feature of this IDE is that it allows you to execute command-line operations in the Galileo's Linux shell. This way, it is possible to print useful information in the Galileo serial connection through the Linux shell, such as the board IP address, and in this particular use case, your CPU temperature.

In this chapter, we will create a bootable SD card, connect our board to the Internet using an Ethernet cable or Wi-Fi, read the Galileo CPU internal temperature sensor, and plot the collected data to an online chart.

 Instructions for both wired and wireless connections will be provided.

In this chapter, we will cover the following topics:

- Burning a Linux bootable image to an SD card
- Booting Galileo from a microSD card
- Connecting to the Internet using a wired or wireless connection
- Using Galileo as a Web Client
- Running Linux shell command-line operations using the Arduino IDE
- Discovering Galileo IP address

- Reading from the internal CPU temperature sensor
- Using the Arduino SD library to read from the SD card
- Plotting the gathered temperature data to an online chart

Booting Galileo from an SD card

Booting your board from an SD card brings you many advantages. Besides allowing you to connect to the Internet from a Wi-Fi connection and have your application memory increased, it makes your Arduino sketches persistent and also allows you the possibility of using more interesting development tools and languages such as Python.

To burn your image, you'll need:

- A FAT32 formatted microSD card. It can be of any size from 1 GB up to 32 GB.
- A computer.
- An SD card adapter (optional).

Let's start by downloading the **Clanton** image which is available at `https://communities.intel.com/community/makers/drivers`; click on the **SD-Card Linux Image** link to start your download.

When the download completes, you'll have to extract its contents.

For extracting the downloaded file in Linux OS, use the following steps:

1. If you don't have `bzip2` already installed, you should install it by typing `sudo apt-get install bzip2` in your terminal.

2. Extract the file contents using the command `bzip2 -cd downloaded_file.tar.bz2 | tar xvf -`, where `downloaded_file.tar.bz2` is your downloaded file.

3. Find the card mounting point by executing the `df -h` command and then insert your card in the card reader and execute the same command again. The new entry in the printed list is your SD card mounting point.

4. Copy the contents of the extracted folder by typing `cp -r * /media/your_mounting_point`, with `/media/your_mounting_point` being the card mounting point that you've found using the `df` command.

To extract the downloaded file on Mac, open the downloaded file with your system compress utility and extract the folder contents to the top of the SD card drive.

To extract the downloaded file in Windows, you can use WinRAR to extract the downloaded file contents and use the following steps:

1. Insert your card in the card reader.

2. When the extraction finishes, copy the extracted folder contents and paste them in the top directory of the SD card volume.

Now, you should have your bootable SD card ready and the root of your SD card will now contain the following files:

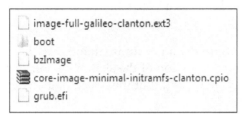

SD card contents

With your Galileo powered off, insert the SD card in the board. You'll need to wait for some time to have the board ready and booted from the SD card.

Now, let's get the board connected to the Internet, so that we can test whether the Galileo had booted properly.

Getting connected to the Internet

Internet access is a must-have in the IoT world. Galileo brings an Ethernet port that allows you to connect to a wired network and in its back, there's also a Mini PCI Express slot where you can attach a Wi-Fi adapter. You are free to choose your connection type, and in the next section, you'll find everything you need to connect your Galileo to the Internet.

Connecting through cable

Connecting to the Internet using the Galileo Ethernet port is pretty simple. All you'll need is an Ethernet cable. Plug one side of the cable to the Galileo and the other side to your network using an available port in your router. You'll be connected right away when you power on your board.

Now, let's test whether you have the Internet access by running a simple Web Client sketch:

1. Power your board with the Ethernet cable plugged in.

2. Open the Arduino IDE and connect your computer to the Galileo using the serial cable.

3. In the **Examples** menu, select the **WebClient** example inside the **Ethernet** tab (**File | Examples | Ethernet | WebClient**).

This is a simple sketch that acts as a Web Client and requests Google to search for the term — Arduino.

Since this example was originally an Arduino demo, we may need to add the following two lines of code at the top of the sketch's setup method to ensure that the network interface is up, and that the board had enough time to start and obtain an IP address:

```
void setup() {
  system("ifup eth0");
  delay(3000);

  // Open serial communications and wait for port to open:
  Serial.begin(9600);

  ...
```

 If you want to read more about the ifup command, you can find more information about it at http://www.linux-tutorial. info/modules.php?name=ManPage&sec=8&manpage=ifup.

Compile and upload the sketch to your board, and open the serial monitor so that you can read the Google server response:

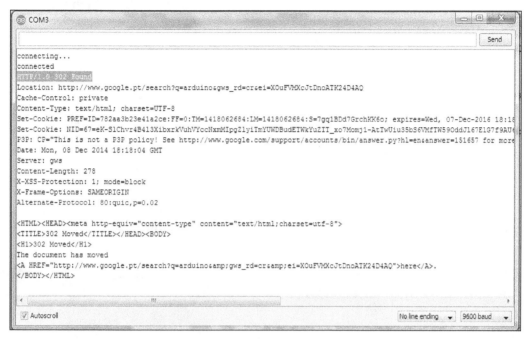

Google server response

Looking at the serial monitor window, you should see the raw HTML response to your request. If you find a response status written in the response (highlighted in the figure), you can consider yourself connected. It doesn't have to be exactly a status code 302 Found; as long as it is written in the debugger, it means that your request reached their servers, and was successfully replied.

Connecting through Wi-Fi

The examples we will cover in this book can work with both cable or wireless Internet connections. If you prefer connecting to the Internet using Wi-Fi, you'll need:

- **MicroSD card**: The Wi-Fi drivers require a considerable amount of memory that won't fit Galileo's available flash memory. You'll need to boot your board using a Linux image. If you haven't burned your bootable Linux image to a microSD card yet, you should do it (instructions are available in the *Booting Galileo from an SD card* section explained earlier in this chapter).

- **A Wi-Fi adapter**: Your SD card Linux image already supports some adapters (supporting both Wi-Fi and Bluetooth), but any Mini PCI Express Wi-Fi card whose drivers exist for Linux should work if you install them. In this book, we'll be using an Intel Centrino Wireless-N 135 card. This wireless card is supported by default.

> If you prefer using a different one, you may find its drivers at `https://wireless.wiki.kernel.org/en/users/Drivers/iwlwifi`.

- **Antennas**: If your Wi-Fi module requires antennas, you'll need to connect at least one to it (`http://uk.mouser.com/ProductDetail/TE-Connectivity/2118060-1/?qs=kOrxwh0XC022OgMI%252bdyLgA==`).

With the Galileo powered off, connect your Wi-Fi adapter to the PCI-E slot located in the backside of the board. In this example, we are using an Intel Centrino Wireless-N 135 card, which can be seen in the following image:

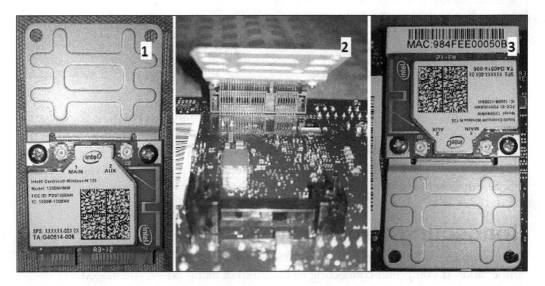

In order to connect your board through Wi-Fi, perform the following steps:

1. Attach the adapter bracket to the mini PCI-E wireless adapter using the screws provided.
2. Insert your Wi-Fi adapter in the Galileo's PCI-E slot.
3. Pull the bottom part of the adapter, until the retention latches are locked inside the holes of the bracket.

4. Also, if your adapter requires antennas, attach them to the respective slots.

5. If you have the Ethernet cable connected, disconnect it and you can now power the board on.

If you are using a different Wi-Fi adapter, you may need to install its drivers.

 For more help on installing drivers, refer to `http://www.malinov.com/Home/sergey-s-blog/intelgalileo-addingwifi`.

Scanning Wi-Fi networks

Open your Arduino IDE and open the sketch **ScanNetworks** located in **File | Examples | WiFi | ScanNetworks**. Just like in the previous wired example, let's add the following system command to the beginning of the setup method to ensure that the `wlan0` network interface is up and running:

```
system("ifup wlan0");
```

Upload it to your Galileo and open the serial monitor. This sketch scans all the available networks in the board's range and prints them into the serial connection. You'll be able to find your network listed in the serial monitor window.

Connecting to the Internet and testing the Wi-Fi connection

Now, let's test the Wi-Fi connection for the Internet access. Open the sketch Wi-Fi Web Client located in **File | Examples | WiFi | WifiWebClient**. At the top of the sketch, you can find the following lines of code:

```
char ssid[] = "yourNetwork"; //  your network SSID (name)
char pass[] = "secretPassword"; // your network password (use for
WPA, or use as key for WEP)
```

You need to replace `yourNetwork` by your network SSID; if your network is visible to everyone, you should select the SSID that was listed in the Wi-Fi scanner sketch. You must also replace `secretPassword` by your network access password.

Also, at the top of your `setup` method, add the lines below to make sure your network interface is ready:

```
system("ifup wlan0");
delay(3000);
```

This sketch will configure your Wi-Fi network access and, like the Ethernet Web Client sketch for the cabled connection, it will try to request a Google search. Upload the sketch to your board, open the serial monitor, and if everything went well, you should see the replied raw HTML; this means that you are properly connected.

Finding your board IP address

Now that you have your board connected, let's find the Galileo IP address. You are free to choose either a wired or a wireless connection, as long as your Galileo has the Internet connection.

There are different ways to discover your board's IP address. One of them is using the Linux `ifconfig` command (`http://ss64.com/bash/ifconfig.html`). It will print your Internet adapters and its properties. With the help of the `system` command, you'll be able to execute Linux instructions from the Arduino IDE. This is a special Galileo command that instructs your Arduino code to execute a command line instruction in the Linux shell. It only takes one parameter—a string with your instruction. Let's create a new sketch:

```
void setup() {
  delay(1000);
  system("ifconfig -a > /dev/ttyGS0");
}

void loop() {}
```

Compile and upload the sketch to your board, and open the serial monitor. This sketch executes the Linux `ifconfig` command, outputting the Galileo network interfaces to the serial port. Standard output and error will be redirected to `/dev/ttyGS0`, which is the device Galileo uses to display information in the serial monitor:

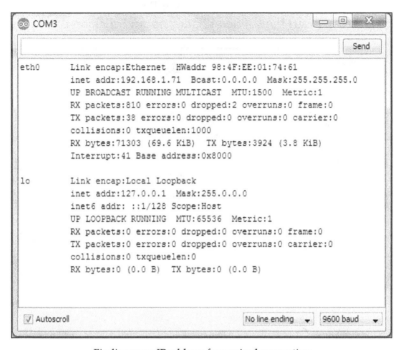

Finding your IP address for a wired connection

In the serial monitor, you'll find all your network interfaces listed. Your wired connection can be read from the `eth0` interface and the Wi-Fi connection from the `wlan0` interface.

Reading the board temperature

Now that you've found your IP address, let's access the board via SSH. Connect your computer to the same network as Galileo. If you are using Linux or Mac OS X, type the following command in your command line, replacing the IP address with the one you've found in the previous step:

```
$  ssh root@192.168.1.71
```

[If you are prompted for the password during the connection process, leave the field empty and press *Enter*.]

If you are using Windows, you should download PuTTY (`http://www.putty.org/`), select the **SSH** option, insert the Galileo IP address, and click on the **Open** button:

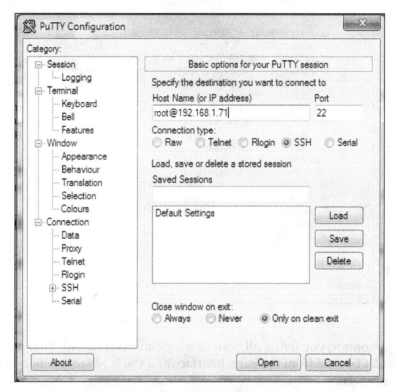

Connecting to the board through SSH using PuTTY

If everything went well, you should now be connected to Galileo via SSH, and see the following shell prompt:

`root@clanton:~$`

This way, you can now confirm that your bootable image is working fine.

Now, let's read the CPU temperature value. As you know, everything in Linux is a file, and the temperature value is no exception. You'll find it in the path `/sys/class/thermal/thermal_zone0/temp`. Running the `cat` command (`http://ss64.com/bash/cat.html`), you'll be able to read the Galileo Quark SoC temperature. To do this, run the following command in the SSH shell:

```
root@clanton:~$ cat /sys/class/thermal/thermal_zone0/temp
```

The command returns the current read value of the Galileo CPU temperature in Celsius:

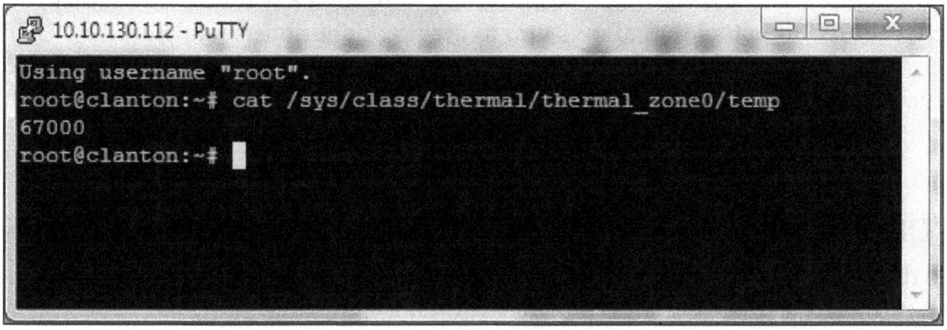

Reading internal temperature value using PuTTY

To obtain the real temperature value, you should divide the read value by 1000, so that we can read it as 67 degree Celsius. This is an expected value, so don't get alarmed; Galileo CPU temperature is usually considerably high. Coming back to the Arduino IDE, you can now read the temperature in the serial console using a system call.

Now, let's try capturing the integer value of the temperature every second by running the following sketch:

```
void setup() {
  Serial.begin(9600);
    delay(1000);
  Serial.println("Started capturing");
}

void loop() {
  Serial.println("reading..");
  system("echo $((`cat /sys/class/thermal/thermal_zone0/temp` / 1000))
> /dev/ttyGS0");
  delay(1000);
}
```

This sketch will run a Linux instruction that retrieves the internal temperature value, divide it by 1000, and output the resulting integer part to the serial port. After uploading the sketch, you should see the temperature values appearing on your serial monitor.

Plotting your temperature data

Now, let's use everything you've learned so far to create temperature data samples and use them to draw an online chart. In this example, we will be using **Plotly**. It is a very useful online tool that allows you to create online charts using an API. Using a free plan, we are able to create unlimited number of public and up to ten private charts. The whole idea of this demo is to capture the temperature values each second during a minute and use the gathered data to create a chart.

Creating temperature data samples

With the `system` command, we were able to print the temperature values to the serial port. This is the right tool to print the data to our serial port, but to be able to use it, we'll need to assign that same data to vars. One way to do this is combining our system calls with the Arduino SD library methods. We need to change the temperature output from the serial port to a path where the SD library can read it. To do so, we can use the following system call:

```
system("echo $((`cat /sys/class/thermal/thermal_zone0/temp` /
1000)) > /media/realroot/sample.tmp");
```

This will print the integer part of the read temperature to the path /media/realroot (which is the SD card path), to the file named sample.tmp.

Now, to read from /media/realroot/sample.tmp, we must use the SD library. Using this library, we'll open the sample file and assign its contents to a String variable. In the following sketch, we'll output the temperature to a file and assign it to a String:

```
#include <SD.h>

void setup() {

  Serial.begin(9600);
  delay(3000); //Give it some time so we can read the prints

  //Read, calculate and store the temperature value in the SD card
```

```
system("echo $((`cat /sys/class/thermal/thermal_zone0/temp` /
1000)) > /media/realroot/sample.tmp");

    //start the SD card
    SD.begin();

    //check if the file exists. It will search inside/media/realroot
    if (SD.exists("sample.tmp")) {

      //Open the File
      File myFile = SD.open("sample.tmp");
      if (myFile) {
        String value;
        while (myFile.available()) {
          value += (char)myFile.read();
        }
       myFile.close();

        //Remove whitespaces
        value.trim();
        Serial.println(value);
      }
    }
  }

  void loop() {}
```

In the serial connection window, you should see the temperature value, which the file contains, printed. This time, the temperature was printed from an Arduino variable and not just outputted directly to the serial port using a command-line instruction. If we use this process in loops, we'll be able to collect multiple samples of data.

Plotting a chart

Now that we found out how to collect temperature samples, let's have a look at the Plotly (`https://plot.ly/`) website to discover how we can use it to plot the temperature over time.

First thing to do is to create an account. Click on the **CREATE ACCOUNT** button. You can register by filling in your name, e-mail, and password or using your favourite social platform account. Now, if you click on the API libraries link, you'll find out that there's an **Arduino** library available, but unfortunately, it has specific Arduino architecture dependencies that won't run in Galileo. Luckily, we have access to the **API Protocol** documentation listed below on the same page.

Plotly has two APIs—a REST API and a Streaming API. The REST API allows us to style and draw online charts with simple HTTP per request/response model, while the Streaming API offers the possibility of updating our charts in real time. In this demo, we will only be using the REST API to plot the Galileo's temperature changes during one minute. If you click on the **REST API** link, you'll be able to see the two available endpoints—one to create a new account, and the other one to create, modify and style graphs. Click on the last endpoint and you'll discover the required query string parameters. So, we'll need to include the following fields in the request:

- `username`: The username you used when creating the Plotly account.
- `API key`: You can find it in the API settings, inside the settings menu.
- `origin`: The type of request we want. We'll stick with the `plot` type.
- `args`: This is where we define the `x` and `y` chart data.
- `kwargs`: These are the other options, such as the filename and chart layout.

The response to the expected request should have a 200 status code, bringing in the payload, a JSON object containing the chart filename and access URL, error (if exists), warning (if exists), and an optional message. Having all this information, we need to configure our Web Client to create such type of requests.

We need to print the following request to the Web Client socket after connecting to Plotly servers:

```
POST /clientresp HTTP/1.1
Host: plotly.ly
User-Agent: Galileo/0.0.1
Content-Length: (needs to be calculated)

version=2.3&origin=plot&platform=Galileo&un=my_username&key=my_api
_key&args={"x":[my_collected_x_values],"y":[my_collected_y_values]
,"type":"scatter","mode":"lines+markers","visible":true}&kwargs={"
filename":"galileo_temperature","fileopt":"overwrite","style":{"ty
pe":"line"},"layout":{"title":"Galileo CPU
Temperature"},"world_readable": true}
```

Now that we have everything we need, let's join the temperature samples gathered with the Plotly Web Client to collect data and plot our chart. Data will be collected sensibly every second for a minute.

 You can download the code for this chapter from the official Packt Publishing website.

Open the Arduino IDE and navigate to **File | Open** and then select the `_6_Wired_TemperatureChart.ino` file from the `_6_Wired_TemperatureChart` folder.

Replace `MY_USERNAME` with your Plotly username, `MY_API_KEY` with your Plotly API key, and the `MAC` address with the one you can find printed in your Ethernet socket. Using an Ethernet connection and your bootable image starts the Galileo board, and uploads the sketch you had just opened.

If you have a look at the code, at the end of `setup`, we are executing a `system` command with the `touch` instruction (`http://ss64.com/bash/touch.html`). This Linux instruction can be used to create a new empty file. If the file doesn't exist by the time this sketch is executed, it will be created when the sketch starts writing read temperatures, ensuring that the file exists.

The `loop` method is split in two parts. Every time a temperature is read, it is added to a String that will contain all the gathered samples. When the counter reaches its limit from 0 to 60 seconds, it will post a request to the Plotly API.

Looking at your serial monitor, you'll see printed the x and y values that are being collected. After posting the data to the Plotly API, you should see a similar response printed:

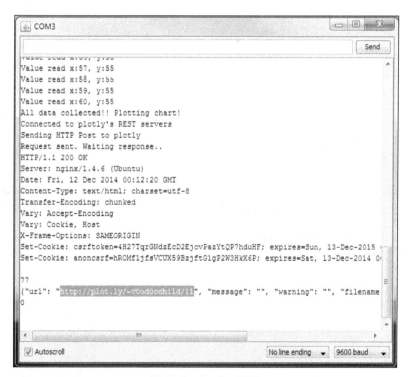

Obtaining the chart URL

Looking at the response, you'll find a JSON key named URL. This URL is where your chart is displayed. Use a web browser to open it and you'll see a chart with your board temperature over one minute of time.

Since your sketch is now persistent because you are using an SD card image, give your Galileo a rest and power it off for 10 minutes. After that time, it should be cooler, so power it on again. The sketch will start automatically. Give your board about a minute to collect the data and plot the chart. After that time, reload your chart web page:

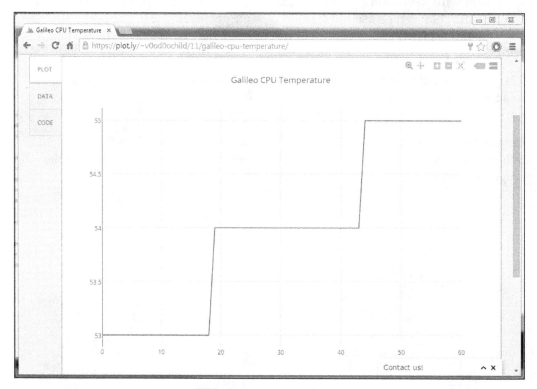

Galileo's temperature increasing

You should now see a different chart with your board's temperature increasing over time.

In this demo, we've used the Ethernet cable connection to connect with Plotly servers. If you wish, you can use a Wi-Fi connection instead. To do this, you'll need to use the Wi-Fi client instead, replacing the beginning of the sketch with the following code:

```
#include <SD.h>
#include <WiFi.h>

char ssid[] = "yourNetwork"; //  your network SSID (name)
char pass[] = "secretPassword"; // your network password (use for
WPA, or use as key for WEP)

int status = WL_IDLE_STATUS;
WiFiClient client;

String username = "MY_USERNAME";
String api_key = "MY_API_KEY";

String temperaturesY = "[";
String timesX = "[";
int seconds = 0;

void setup() {
  system("ifup wlan0");
  delay(1000);
  Serial.begin(9600);
  while (status != WL_CONNECTED) {
    Serial.print("Attempting to connect to SSID: ");
    Serial.println(ssid);
    // Connect to WPA/WPA2 network. Change this line if using open
or WEP network:
    status = WiFi.begin(ssid, pass);

    // wait 10 seconds for connection:
    delay(10000);
  }
  Serial.println("Connected to wifi");

  Serial.println("Starting SD card...");
  if (!SD.begin()) {
    Serial.println("SD card failed to start!");
    return;
  }
  Serial.println("SD card started successfuly");
```

```
    delay(5000);
    system("touch /media/realroot/sample.tmp");
}
```

...

As a challenge, you can always extend this demo to use the Plotly Streaming API and enable real-time updates in your chart, making the data collection step much lighter, allowing the board to plot for a huge time amount.

Summary

Galileo can connect to the Internet using its Ethernet or Wi-Fi adapter. To do so, you've learned how to build and boot the board from a *bigger* Linux image through an SD card, which uses Wi-Fi drivers and makes sketches persist when the board reboots. Also, you've learned how to execute Linux commands from the Arduino IDE, finding your IP address, and reading the CPU temperature. You used the SD library to be able to collect temperature samples, and finally created a Web Client that is able to plot charts.

In the next chapter, you'll learn how to develop a motion sensing light using the Arduino IDE.

4
Creating a Motion Sensing Light

In many public buildings, house gardens, or even common spaces such as restrooms, we can find lights that are triggered on when motion or presence is detected. These kinds of systems aim to save electricity by turning the lights on only when they are needed, not giving the chance of someone forgetting to turn them off.

In this chapter, we will create our own energy saving lighting system. We'll control a single AC powered lightbulb using a solid state relay, which will be operated by the Galileo considering sensorial data. You'll learn how to use the Arduino IDE to read digital and analog data from sensors. Finally, we'll build a web server to serve a web page, allowing you to control the whole system with it.

In this chapter, we will cover the following topics:

- Reading analog and digital inputs with the Arduino IDE
- Learning how to use a PIR sensor for motion detection
- Learning how to use a photoresistor to detect luminosity
- Controlling a solid state relay considering the collected data from sensors
- Using Galileo as a web server
- Controlling the whole system using a web page served by Galileo

Required equipment

This project will require some electronic and electrical equipment. We'll be building not only DC, but also AC circuits.

> If you don't feel comfortable building the circuits yourself, please seek the help of someone more experienced to ensure that the circuits are built properly and are safe to use.

To be able to complete all the steps in this chapter, besides the Galileo board, you'll need the following material:

- A lightbulb, a lightbulb socket, and a power plug:

In this example, we'll be using an E27 lightbulb (220 V-240 V, 20 W, 160 mA) with the correspondent socket and a power plug. We'll be using a European C-type plug, supporting 220 V. If you want to use another type of plug, socket, or lightbulb, be sure that they are compatible, otherwise you'll need to do some adjustments to the circuits.

- A Passive infrared motion sensor:

For the motion detection, we'll be using a generic HC-SR501 **Passive Infrared (PIR)** motion sensor supporting 5 V. This type of sensor can detect motion by measuring heat changes in its surroundings.

 If you need to purchase one, visit http://www.amazon. com/Great-Deal-HC-SR501-Infrared-Raspberry/ dp/B00M1H7KBW.

- A photoresistor and a 10 kΩ resistor:

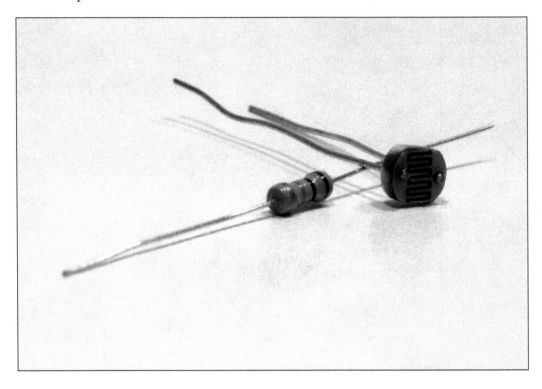

The photoresistor is a special type of resistor with a photoconductive property. The resistor value changes depending on the amount of light it is exposed to. It is a cheap option and a great addition to obtain input on the day's luminosity. You'll also need a resistor for the circuit. We'll use a 10 kΩ resistor, which is represented by the colors: brown, black, orange, and gold.

If you need to purchase a photoresistor and a 10 kΩ resistor, you can order them at `http://www.ebay.com/itm/3-x-Light-Photosensitive-Detector-Sensor-Switch-LDR-3-x-10k-Resistor-Arduino-/181585094020?hash=item2a4750a584`.

- A solid state relay, four two-core cable and Y terminals:

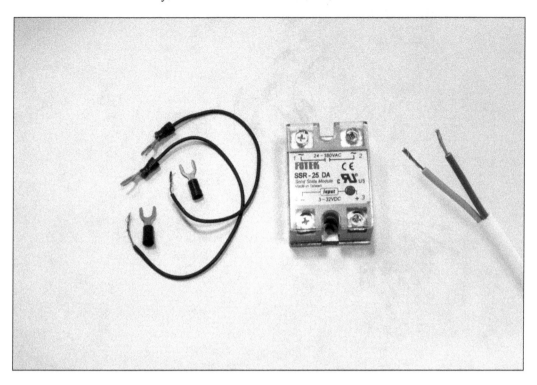

To be able to control a 220 V lightbulb, we'll need to use a relay. A relay is a switch that is electrically controlled. It uses an electromagnet to mechanically pull two connections together and close that circuit. In this particular case, we will be using a solid state relay. It is also a switch, but it doesn't contain mechanical parts. Besides having a bigger lifetime than the electromechanical relay, it is safer to operate, considerably faster, but more expensive. We'll need one solid state relay (`http://www.amazon.com/Bessky-TM-White-Controller-24-380V/dp/B00HIU8TSK`) that can handle 220 V AC, being operated by 5 V DC. We'll also need a two-core cable (`http://www.ebay.com/itm/2-Core-6A-Black-Power-Cable-0-75mm-Electric-Flexible-Mains-Car-Wire-/360465655261`) long enough to connect the lightbulb socket to the relay and power plug. Using Y terminals (`http://www.amazon.com/Absolute-USA-ST1210Y-Insulated-Connectors/dp/B00M4CZZJI`) in the cables that will be connected to the relay will help make the wiring process easier and safer.

- A breadboard and some jumper wires:

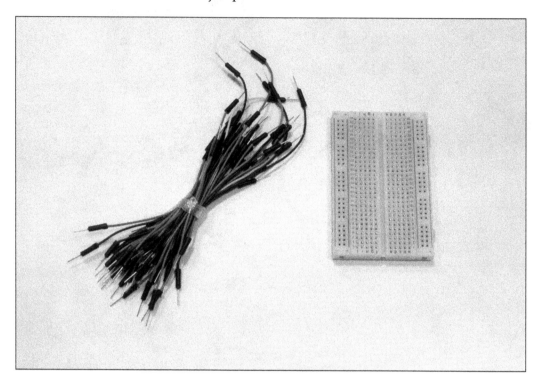

A small breadboard and a couple of male/male hookup wires will help you connect your sensors to the Galileo.

 If you need to purchase them, you can find them at http://www.amazon.com/microtivity-IB401-400-point-Experiment-Breadboard/dp/B004RXKWDQ.

Controlling a lightbulb

Before starting to wire the circuit, keep in mind that you'll be using 220 V AC and there's a risk of electrocution. It can be very dangerous to use high voltages if some precautions aren't taken into consideration.

During the whole wiring process, ensure that your circuit is not connected to the wall socket.

Always keep your circuit disconnected from the wall socket when wiring or changing the circuit.

Isolate the AC part of the circuit. It is the best way to avoid touching exposed wires accidently.

 Be extremely careful when wiring the AC component of the circuit. Use the Y terminals to connect the wires to the relay and do not let there be any exposed wire that you may accidently touch.

If you have any doubt or you are not sure what to do, ask a more experienced person for help.

 If you want to read more about solid state relay safety precautions, visit at http://www.omron.com/ecb/products/pdf/ precautions_ssr.pdf.

Keeping this in mind, let's start assembling our circuit:

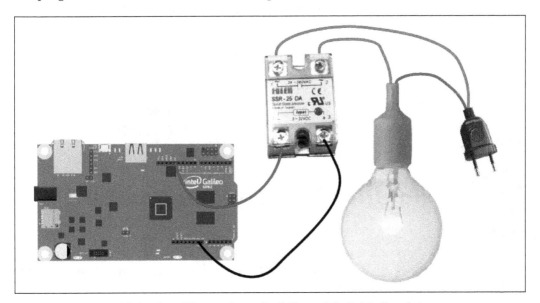

Wiring the solid state relay to the Galileo and the lightbulb socket

The blue wire in the diagram represents the neutral. You should connect it to the neutral connector of the lightbulb socket, which should be located at the bottom of the bulb socket. Connect the other end of the wire to the power plug.

The two brown wires in the diagram represent the hot. Connect the first brown cable between the lightbulb socket's hot connector and the relay connector number 2, in the AC component of the relay. Connect the second brown cable between the power plug and the relay connector number 1, also in the AC part of the relay.

Grab your Galileo board. Connect one jumper wire from pin 13 to the solid state relay connector number 3 (plus sign) in the DC component and the Galileo's ground to the relay's connector 4 (minus sign).

Be sure that you have your circuit similar to the preceding schematic image, especially the AC components.

 You'll need to be **extremely careful** when using the circuit. Don't ever touch it when the power plug is connected to the wall socket. If you need to do adjustments, first disconnect it from the wall socket.

With your AC circuit disconnected from the wall socket, open the Arduino IDE. To test our circuit, let's use the **Blink** sketch. Open the sketch by navigating to **File | Examples | Basics | Blink**. As you've seen earlier, this sketch changes the pin status to its complement every second. Since this pin is now connected to the solid state relay, setting the pin value to HIGH will activate the relay, turning the lightbulb on. Setting the pin value to LOW will deactivate the relay, turning the lightbulb off.

In the sketch code, confirm that you are using pin 13:

```
int led = 13;
```

Connect your power plug to a wall socket and upload the sketch to your Galileo. You should now see your lightbulb blinking. The relay only supports the on and off status; don't try to fade the lightbulb as it won't work.

Controlling the relay using a motion sensor

A simple way to detect motion is using a PIR sensor. This sensor measures infrared light radiation emitted by the objects in its range. By detecting changes in the amount of radiation, it can detect motion.

 Before starting to do the changes in the circuit, disconnect your AC plug from the wall socket.

Using the relay circuit from the previous step and having the AC plug disconnected from the socket, add the following connections:

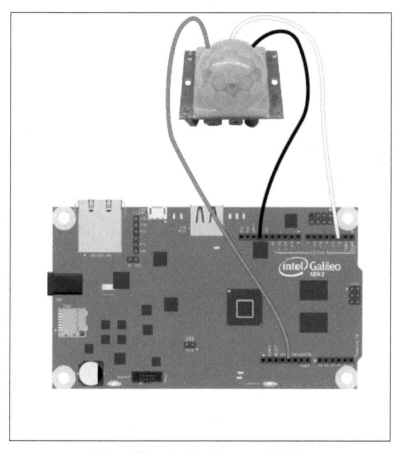

Wiring a PIR motion detection sensor to Galileo

Your PIR sensor should have three pins. Be sure to connect its VCC pin to the Galileo's 5 V pin, the GND pin to the Galileo's ground, and the OUT pin to the Galileo's pin 2. Whenever the sensor detects motion, we'll be able to read the value HIGH on the Galileo's pin 2. When the sensor stops detecting, we'll be able to read LOW.

Open the Arduino IDE, power on your Galileo (just the Galileo, not the lightbulb plug), and upload the following code:

```
// Pin where we will read the sensor data
int pir_data_pin = 2;
// Pin which we will use to control the relay
int relay_pin = 13;   // Initializing PIR status as low
```

```
int last_pir_status = LOW;

void setup() {
  pinMode(relay_pin, OUTPUT);
  // Set pin as input so we can read it
  pinMode(pir_data_pin, INPUT);    digitalWrite(pir_data_pin,
LOW);
  Serial.begin(9600);
  Serial.print("Calibrating sensor ");

  //Give the sensor 20 seconds to warm up and calibrate
  for(int i = 0; i < 20; i++){
    Serial.print(".");
    delay(1000);
  }

  Serial.println("Sensor ready!");
 }

// Set relay status
void setLightbulbStatus(int status) {
  digitalWrite(relay_pin, status);
}

void loop(){
  if(digitalRead(pir_data_pin) == HIGH){

    // If transition is from LOW to HIGH
    //motion was detected, activate the relay
    if (last_pir_status == LOW) {
      Serial.println("Motion detected");

     // Activate the relay
      setLightbulbStatus(HIGH);

      // Set status to the current one
      last_pir_status = HIGH;
    }

  } else {

    // If transition is from HIGH to LOW
    //motion stopped being detected, deactivate the relay
    if (last_pir_status == HIGH){
```

```
        Serial.println("Motion stopped");

        // Deactivate the relay
        setLightbulbStatus(LOW);

        // Set status to the current one
        last_pir_status = LOW;
      }
    }
    delay(50);
}
```

Because of the way this kind of sensor works (heat), when the Galileo is powered, we first need to let the sensor calibrate with its surroundings for at least 20 seconds. After this, the PIR should be ready. Open the serial monitor, and every time you move you should see the triggered event printed and the on-board LED turning on when motion is detected and turning off when motion stops being sensed.

If you are struggling to trigger the sensor, you will find two potentiometers in it. One tagged as *Sx* and another as *Tx*. The *Sx* potentiometer allows you to adjust the sensor's sensibility, while the *Tx* allows you to adjust the output time. Use a Philips screwdriver to adjust them until you start obtaining more responsiveness. Having a look at the code, in the `loop` method, we are filtering the transitions from HIGH to LOW, and vice versa.

This way, we will be able to manipulate the relay properly, turning the lightbulb on/off when there is the correspondent transition. Plug in the lighthulb plug to the wall socket and with the Galileo powered on, upload the sketch. Wait for the sensor calibration to finish, and then give it a try by waving at the sensor. Combining the PIR logic with the preceding relay control code, the lightbulb will be turned on when motion is detected.

Detecting luminosity

In the previous step, you saw how to use a PIR motion sensor to control a relay. That is interesting when it's dark, but during the daylight you'll have a waste of energy with the lightbulb being turned on. Keeping this in mind, let's improve our lighting circuit to only let the lightbulb turn on when the incident amount of light (luminosity) is low. To do so, we'll add a photoresistor to our circuit.

Photoresistors are light-dependent resistors. The incisive amount of light will define the resistor value. By using them, we are able to understand when it is night or day by setting the threshold values. Unplug your bulb plug from the wall socket and let's do some changes in our circuit. In the following figure, you can see how you must connect the photoresistor to the Galileo:

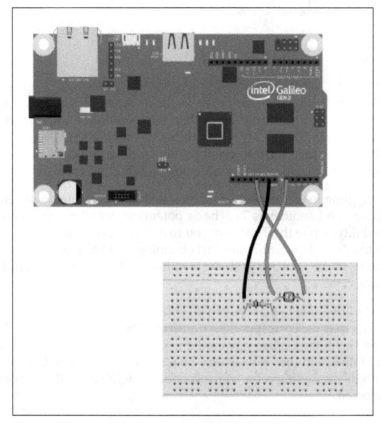

Wiring a photoresistor to Galileo

One side of the photoresistor should be connected to the 5 V pin. To the other side, we must connect the resistor and wire it to the Galileo's pin A0 using a jumper wire. To close the circuit, we must connect the end of the resistor to the Galileo's ground.

Now that you have seen how you should wire it, let's add the photoresistor to our lighting circuit. Our circuit should look similar to the following:

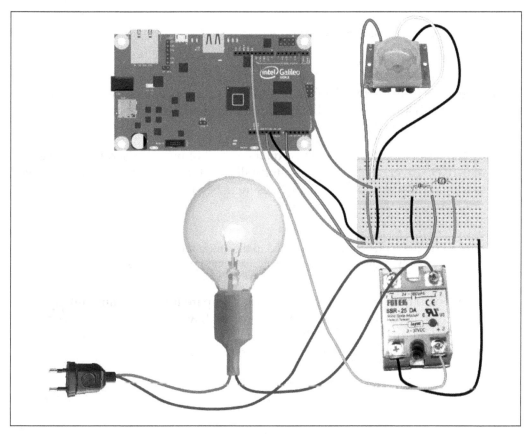

Complete wiring diagram with bulb, relay, PIR sensor and photoresistor

Open the Arduino IDE and let's find out what we can read from the A0 pin by uploading the following sketch; do not plug the AC power plug to the wall socket yet:

```
// To this pin is connected the photoresistor and a 10K pulldown
resistor
int photoresistor_pin = 0;
// The analog reading from the sensor divider
int photoresistor_reading;
void setup(void) {
  Serial.begin(9600);
}

void loop(void) {
  // Read from the analog pin A0
```

```
Photoresistor_reading = analogRead(photoresistorPin);
Serial.print("PhotoValue reading = ");
// the raw analog reading

Serial.println(photoresistor_reading);
delay(100);
}
```

The Galileo pins from A0 to A5 are analog pins. To read its values, we must use the `analogRead` method. This method maps input voltages between 0 and 5 volts into integer values between 0 and 1023.

Opening the serial monitor of the IDE, you'll see a lot of numbers scrolling in the range of 0-1023. Covering the photoresistor will result in the read values going lower and exposing it to light will make the values increase. Those values you see printed can be interpreted as the amount of light.

 This is a raw read value related to the amount of light and is not directly related to lumens or any other kind of light measurement unit.

All we need to do here is to set a threshold and compare it with the amount of light that is read. If the read value is below threshold, we can consider this scenario acceptably dark to turn on our lightbulb. Let's give it a try. Connect the power plug to the wall socket and upload the following sketch to your Galileo:

```
// PIR variables
int pir_data_pin = 2;
int last_pir_status = LOW;

// Relay variables
int relay_pin = 13;

// Photoresistor variables
int photoresistor_pin = 0;
int photoresistor_value;

// Define your threshold value
int light_treshold = 400;

void setup() {
  pinMode(relay_pin, OUTPUT);
  // Set pin as input so we can read it
  pinMode(pir_data_pin, INPUT);
  digitalWrite(pir_data_pin, LOW);
  Serial.begin(9600);
```

```
  Serial.print("Calibrating sensor ");

  //Give PIR sensor 20 seconds to warm up and calibrate
  for (int i = 0; i < 20; i++) {
    Serial.print(".");
    delay(1000);
  }
  Serial.println("Sensor ready!");
}

void setLightBulbStatus(int status) {
  digitalWrite(relay_pin, status);
}

// returns true if "dark"
boolean isDark() {
  photoresistor_value = analogRead(photoresistor_pin);
  Serial.print("Ammount of light = ");
  Serial.println(photoresistor_value);
  return (photoresistor_value < light_treshold);
}

void controlLightWithMotionSensor() {
  if (digitalRead(pir_data_pin) == HIGH) {
    if (last_pir_status == LOW) {
      Serial.println("Motion start");
      setLightBulbStatus(HIGH);
      last_pir_status = HIGH;
    }

  } else {
    if (last_pir_status == HIGH) {
      Serial.println("Motion stopped");
      setLightBulbStatus(LOW);
      last_pir_status = LOW;
    }
  }
}

void loop(){
  //When is dark, check if motion was detected
  if (isDark()) {
    controlLightWithMotionSensor();
  }
  delay(50);
}
```

In this sketch, we changed a couple of things to help make it easier to read. We moved the code that controls the lightbulb using the motion sensor inside the `void` method `controlLightWithMotionSensor`.

In the `loop` method, we will now be repeatedly calling the `isDark` verifier. We are testing whether the raw amount of light value that is being read is below our threshold. The motion sensor will only control the light when that condition is fulfilled.

Using Galileo as a web server

So far, we were able to control our lightbulb using sensors. Now, let's try to display our sensorial data in a web page. To do so, we will use the Galileo as a web server and use some common web technologies.

A web server is an application capable of serving, storing, and processing web pages in the Internet or a local network. Browsers are user agents that communicate with web servers through the HTTP protocol, requesting pages' content and displaying it. Typically, a page content contains an HTML document, including images, CSS stylesheets, and client-side JavaScript code. The web server should reply to such requests with the requested web page content, if available, and the user is allowed to access that same content.

Make sure your board has Internet access, either through Wi-Fi or a wired connection. The web server we'll create will only be available in your local network. The first thing we must do is to discover our Galileo's IP address by running the sketch we've already used in the *Finding your board IP address* section in *Chapter 3, Monitoring the Board Temperature*.

Open the Arduino IDE. If you are connecting to the Internet using a wired connection, open the **WebServer** example located in **File | Examples | Ethernet | WebServer**. If you chose to use the wireless connection, open **WiFiWebServer** instead, located in **File | Examples | WiFi | WiFiWebServer**.

Both sketches will be launching a web server that will be listening to client requests (which will be made by our browser) and it will respond to all of them with an HTML page printing the values read from all the analog pins at the time the request was made.

At the beginning of your sketch, you'll need to do the following initial configuration:

- **Ethernet connection**: Replace the MAC and IP addresses with your own values:

```
byte mac[] = {  0xDE, 0xAD, 0xBE, 0xEF, 0xFE, 0xED };
IPAddress ip(192,168,1,177);
```

- **Wi-Fi connection**: Assign your network SSID and password to the correspondent variables:

```
char ssid[] = "yourNetwork";      // your network SSID
(name)
char pass[] = "secretPassword";   // your network password
```

Remove the AC plug from the wall socket, as we won't need it now. Upload the sketch you have just opened and, in your preferred browser, type `http://`, followed by your Galileo IP address (for example, `http://192.168.1.177`).

In the browser, behind the scenes you'll be doing a GET request to the server with the IP address you inserted and to the root path ("/") of the Galileo server.

While receiving the HTTP request, the Galileo web server should respond with a 200 OK status code and the web page HTML content, where you should see the read values from the analog printed. In the displayed pin A0 output, you will find the value that was read from the photoresistor at that particular time.

With this sketch, you were able to display all the analog pins' values read at the request time. To obtain more updated values, you would need to refresh the page constantly because the printed values in the web page will never be updated without a new request. To be able to update the read values on the website, we can use AJAX (Asynchronous JavaScript and XML) requests to fetch data periodically and update the web page fields using JavaScript. Such type of operation is known as **polling**.

Now, let's turn our attention to the web page we want to be served. We want it to be able to not only display the lightbulb status, but also to control it. We'll need one box that represents the light status; three buttons, one for each operation; and a span where we'll be placing the updated values.

 You can refer to `http://jsfiddle.net/` as it will help you edit the HTML, CSS and JavaScript components easily. Put the components on the right boxes and press the **Run** button to be able to view the output of the web page.

The following HTML and CSS styling rules should provide the basic structure we'll need:

```
<!DOCTYPE html>
<html>
    <head>
        <title>My homemade lighting system</title>
        <style type="text/css">
            .bulb {
                width: 200px;
```

```
          height: 200px;
          border: 1px solid black;
          background-color: white;
        }

        .button {
          padding: 15px;
          margin-bottom: 5px;
          border: 1px solid;
          width: 60px;
          text-align: center;
          cursor: pointer;
        }
      </style>
  </head>
  <body>
      <div id="lightbulb1" class="bulb"></div>

      <br/><br/>
      <p>Mode: <span id="light_mode">Unknown</span></p>
      <br/><br/>
      <div class="button">ON</div>
      <div class="button">OFF</div>
      <div class="button">AUTO</div>
  </body>
</html>
```

This page will be served to you by the Galileo and will be displayed in your browser. This is a very simple structure with very poor styling just to fit our needs. Feel free to improve it.

 If you want to learn more about using CSS, take a look at http://www.w3schools.com/css/ and for HTML, visit http://www.w3schools.com/html/.

Now that we have the page structure and style, let's add some logic to this web page using JavaScript. We need to develop a client method that will be executed by your browser, polling the Galileo's web server.

We'll need to make the web server respond to the following requests:

- GET lightbulb_status: This endpoint will return the lightbulb status

- POST status_manual_on: This will force the lightbulb to turn on and ignore the motion detector/photoresistor values

- **POST** `status_manual_off`: This will force the lightbulb to turn off, ignoring the motion detector/photoresistor values
- **POST** `status_auto`: This will use the motion detector circuit input to control the lightbulb automatically

To poll the Galileo web server, we'll be using the AJAX. This is a web development technique that we can use to allow our browser to perform asynchronous requests (in the background) to our web server. This client-side code will be served by the Galileo web server, but it will be running in the browser.

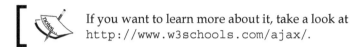 If you want to learn more about it, take a look at `http://www.w3schools.com/ajax/`.

Now, let's take a look on how we can use it to accomplish our objective:

```
function getLightbulbStatus() {

  // Create a new AJAX request
  var request = new XMLHttpRequest();

  //Do not let the AJAX request be cached by adding unique nocache
id
  var noCache = "&nocache=" + Math.random() * 1000000;

  /** Handle the ready state value changes
        0: request not initialized
        1: server connection established
        2: request received
        3: processing request
        4: request finished and response is ready  ready */

  request.onreadystatechange = function () {

    // If response is ready and status code is 200 OK
    if (request.readyState == 4 && request.status == 200 &&
request.responseText != null) {

      // If lightbulb is on
      if (request.responseText.trim() == '1') {
        document.getElementById("lightbulb").style.
backgroundColor="yellow
";
      } else {
```

```
            document.getElementById("lightbulb").style.
        backgroundColor="white"
    ;
            }
        }
    }
    request.open("GET", "lightbulb_status" + noCache, true);
    request.send();

    // Repeat itself in 800ms
    setTimeout(getLightbulbStatus, 800);
      }

function setBulbModeStatus(mode_status) {
    // Create a new AJAX request
    var request = new XMLHttpRequest();
    // Do not let browser cache the request
    var noCache = "&nocache=" + Math.random() * 1000000;
    request.onreadystatechange = function () {

        // If response is ready and status code is 200 OK
        if (request.readyState == 4 && request.status == 200 &&
    request.responseText != null) {
            document.getElementById("light_mode").innerHTML =
    request.status;
        }
    }
    request.open("POST", mode_status + noCache, true);
    request.send();
      }
```

Having a look at the preceding code, we'll have two types of requests. One for polling the lightbulb status handled by the getLightbulbStatus method, and the other for setting the lightbulb operating mode, handled by the setBulbModeStatus method. Every time a request to obtain the lightbulb status is made and a response is obtained, a new timer will be launched. When this timer expires, a new request will be made again, repeating this process forever. The request to change the lightbulb operating mode will only happen whenever a button is pressed.

In the HTML buttons, we can define the action to be called on a click event by the following code:

```
<div id="status_manual_on" class="button"
onclick="setBulbModeStatus(this.id)">ON</div>
<div id="status_manual_off" class="button"
onclick="setBulbModeStatus(this.id)">OFF</div>
<div id="status_auto" class="button"
onclick="setBulbModeStatus(this.id)">AUTO</div>
```

The AJAX script must be included in the served HTML document, inside `<script>` tags, and preferentially, in the `<head>` section so that it can be loaded before the events that will require it.

Going back to the server side, we'll need to have a method that will handle those AJAX requests:

```
void handleResponse (EthernetClient client) {
  // Replying to the client, informing it is a successful request
  client.println("HTTP/1.1 200 OK");
  client.println("Content-Type: text/html");
  client.println("Connection: keep-alive");
  client.println();

  // if the AJAX request is a GET lightbulb_status
   if (request.indexOf("lightbulb_status") > -1) {
     client.println(digitalRead(relay_pin));

  // if the AJAX request is to turn the lightbulb on
  } else if (request.indexOf("status_manual_on") > -1){
    // Activate the relay
    setLightBulbStatus(HIGH);
    client.println("Manual");

  // if the AJAX request is to turn the lightbulb off
  } else if (request.indexOf("status_manual_off") > -1){
     // Deactivate the relay
     setLightBulbStatus(LOW);
     client.println("Manual");

  // if the AJAX request is to control the lightbulb using the
sensors
  } else if (request.indexOf("status_auto") > -1){
    int last_pir_status = LOW;
    setLightBulbStatus(LOW);
```

```
          client.println("Motion Detection");

      // Any other request will be responded with our webpage
      } else {
        printWebPage(client);
      }
  }
```

Every time the `loop` method reads a valid and complete request, it will call the `handleResponse` method, which will search for patterns in the requested URL. Whenever a match is made with the help of the `indexOf` method, it will process the correspondent request. If it is a `lightbulb_status` request, we'll be reading the current relay pin status. If it is a `status_manual_on/off` request, it will operate the relay, and if it is a `status_auto` request, the lightbulb will start being controlled by the sensors. When no match pattern is found, the default web page will be served.

Now that you are a bit more familiarized with the concepts behind this approach, let's see it in action.

 To Download the code files of this chapter, visit the official website of Packt Publishing.

Open the sketch (using the Arduino IDE) `_5_Wired_Polling.ino` from the `_5_ Wired_Polling` folder if you are using a wired Internet connection, or `_5_WiFi_ Polling.ino` from the `_5_WiFi_Polling` folder if you are using a Wi-Fi connection.

 Keep your circuit connected to the Galileo, but the lightbulb disconnected from the wall socket.

Upload the sketch to your board and open the serial monitor. The PIR sensor will be calibrating for about 20 seconds. When it is ready, you'll be able to read `Sensor ready!` in the serial monitor. Connect your computer to the same network as the Galileo. Open your browser and in the URL bar type `http://galileo_ip_address`, replacing `galileo_ip_address` with your board's IP address. After pressing *Enter*, the Galileo will serve you the following web page:

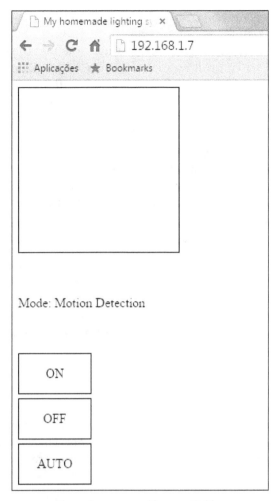

The webpage served by your Galileo

This interface allows you to set the lightbulb status **ON** and **OFF** manually or to change its operation mode to auto, where the lightbulb status will change using the photoresistor and PIR sensor inputs. Click on **AUTO** and try firing the sensor. You may need to change your `light_treshold` variable in the sketch to be more permissive.

When the sensor detects motion and the incident light is below the defined threshold, the rectangle in the top of the page turns yellow. This change is a result of our polling, repeatedly requesting the light status. Note that the onboard LED will also turn on, since we are controlling the relay with the pin 13 and it will be changing its status a little bit before the website's light representation. When a lightbulb status change happens, we won't have an immediate response because we are not being directly informed by the server. Instead, we are asking the Galileo repeatedly what its current status is. The responsiveness will increase a bit if we decrease the time between the requests, but will also put more weight on our server. You can use two modes to turn the lightbulb on—manual or using motion detection. You have already seen what the motion detection mode does. The manual mode will ignore the sensor code and just turn on/off lightbulb when you click on the buttons. If you use the browser developer tools for the network requests monitoring, you'll see a lot of AJAX requests being made in the background. We are querying the Galileo every 800 milliseconds to give us the lightbulb status.

Now, let's plug the lightbulb plug to the wall socket and give it a try testing the created operation modes. A better option to make the system more responsive could be using server notification, possibly using web sockets. With a bit of tweaking and further development, you can add more lightbulbs to the system or even control other devices using relays.

Summary

As you were able to test by yourself, Galileo can be used as a small web server, being able to deliver web pages and callable endpoints. This type of server can be used to allow controlling actuators or display values that are read from the sensors in a local network.

You learned how to use a relay to control a lightbulb. Adjusting the code a bit, you will be able to control your own home lights from a computer or even a mobile device web browser. Besides lightbulbs, relays can be used to control devices such as power outlets or any other devices that have an on and off status.

Using a motion sensor and a photoresistor, you were able to understand how to make the relay actuate based on motion detection and incident light. Although we are used to see motion detection sensors heavily bounded to common spaces' lighting systems, such as entrance halls, it can also be used as a trigger in surveillance or intrusion alarm systems. Photoresistors can also have many more applications. An example can be a gardening watering system, which can use the light information to decide when the lawn should be watered.

While developing a web server to monitor and control the whole system, you came in contact with some basic web development concepts — building a simple webpage and styling it. Using AJAX, you learned how to use short polling, being able to update your web page elements without having to reload them, but with the cost of some delay. In the chapters ahead, you'll be able to explore other technologies that will help you increase your systems responsiveness.

In the next chapter, we'll be leaving the Arduino IDE and we will start exploring the Linux side of the Galileo and Intel Development Kit, discovering what it brings and how it can help you build more complex IoT projects.

5
Intel IoT Developer Kit Tools

So far, you have learned how to develop projects for your Galileo board using the Arduino IDE. If you were already familiar with Arduino boards, you certainly noticed some resemblances developing between both the boards. Although very simple and intuitive to use, it can get complex when you want to develop bigger and more ambitious projects. Also, many developers aren't that keen on developing their projects using the Arduino C/C++ language.

In this chapter, we'll have a look at other available development tools and languages by exploring some of the features that the Intel® IoT Developer Kit pack provides. Being a complete hardware and software solution, it offers way more tools for your IoT projects than the Arduino IDE, also allowing you to develop your projects in other languages and the possibility of using a cloud-based IoT analytics system.

By the end of this chapter, you'll have some notions of what you can use to help you develop your projects by learning how to manipulate your board I/O pins, and extract meaningful data from your sensors using your favorite development language.

In this chapter, you'll learn about:

- The Intel® IoT Developer Kit concept
- Setting up and booting from your IoT Developer Kit image
- Reading from Galileo I/O pins using the Intel MRAA library
- Using the Intel UPM library to read meaningful data from sensors
- Creating and using Node.js, Python, and C++ apps to read data from sensors

Required equipment

In this and the upcoming chapters, we'll be using the Grove Starter Kit Plus—Intel IoT edition sensors. It is a set of sensors that are officially compatible with both Intel Galileo and Intel Edison. For Galileo, there are two kits available. One for Gen 1 (http://www.seeedstudio.com/depot/Grove-starter-kit-plus-Intel-IoT-Edition-for-Intel-Galileo-Gen-1-p-1977.html) and another for Gen 2 (http://www.seeedstudio.com/depot/Grove-starter-kit-plus-Intel-IoT-Edition-for-Intel-Galileo-Gen-2-p-1978.html). Pick the right one for the board you are using.

For this chapter, we'll need:

- **Base Shield V2**: It is an expansion header containing multiple Grove connectors. It allows us to connect multiple Grove sensors to it, allowing us to keep using the expansion header:

- **Light sensor**: Just like the photoresistor we used in the previous chapter, it also detects the intensity of the incident light by decreasing its resistance value when the incident amount of light increases. With the increase in the incident light, the sensor resistance decreases. The main difference is that this sensor packs all the components together and is compatible with the Intel® IoT Developer Kit libraries.

IoT Developer Kit components

Intel® IoT Developer Kit is a complete solution for creating IoT applications for the Intel® Galileo and Intel® Edison boards. It is mainly comprised of:

- **Hardware components**: The hardware components refer to the development board (Intel® Galileo Gen 1, Intel® Galileo Gen 2, and Intel® Edison), sensors, and actuators.

- **Software image**: The Galileo IoT Developer Kit image is a Yocto-embedded Linux-based operating system. It's a bootable image that also includes some of the available Wi-Fi and Bluetooth drivers, but unlike the image we used earlier, it supports a wide range of Linux tools such as the GCC toolchain (http://elinux.org/Toolchains) and libraries such as MRAA (https://github.com/intel-iot-devkit/mraa) and UPM (https://github.com/intel-iot-devkit/upm). This image also supports the Git-distributed version control system (https://git-scm.com/), making it possible to push and pull your code to or from online repositories such as GitHub (https://github.com). The **redis** client (http://redis.io/) is another interesting tool that was made available, allowing developers to use a simple key value cache and storage system. This image also supports code development in C++, Python, and Node.js.

- **IDE and programming language**: You can develop your applications using different Integrated Development Environments. Besides the Arduino IDE, you can use Wyliodrin, the Intel® XDK IoT Edition, and the Eclipse IDE. Wyliodrin (`https://www.wyliodrin.com`) allows you to develop from a web browser using Visual Programming, Python, and Node.js. The Intel® XDK IoT Edition (`https://software.intel.com/en-us/html5/xdk-iot`) allows you to develop your onboard apps using JavaScript (Node.js) and the possibility of building mobile companion apps for your projects. Finally, there is the popular Eclipse IDE, recommended by Intel®, to be used in your C++ projects.

- **Cloud analytics**: For getting your data online, you have now the Intel® IoT cloud analytics (`https://dashboard.us.enableiot.com`) available, where you'll be able to store and analyze the data that is collected by your sensors. It also allows you to create rules that will trigger alerts based on the analyzed data.

Building the image

Let's start by building the IoT Developer Kit image. For this, you'll only need a computer with an SD card reader and a blank 4 GB microSD card. Feel free to pick the SD card size up to the maximum supported size of 32 GB.

Download the latest image version from `http://iotdk.intel.com/images/iot-devkit-latest-mmcblkp0.direct.bz2`. Once the download finishes, enter the downloaded file folder. Depending on the operating system you are using, follow the following correspondent instructions to build your bootable image:

- **Linux**: On a Linux platform, go through the following steps to extract and build an image:

    1. Extract the image file by using the **bunzip2** tool. Open the terminal, navigate to the downloaded file folder, and type the following command:

       `bunzip2 iot-devkit-latest-mmcblkp0.direct.bz2`

    2. Use the `sudo fdisk -1` command to locate your SD card in the file system. If you are not sure which one it is, execute the command with and without the SD card placed in the reader. It will be the entry that only appears once after executing both the commands (for example, `/dev/sdb1`).

    3. With the SD card in the reader, execute the `sudo umount /dev/sdb1`, command where `/dev/sdb1` is the device you found using the command in the previous step.

4. Finally, copy the image to the SD card with the `sudo dd if=iotdk-galileo-image of=/dev/sdb1` command. The `if` part of the command is the path to the target image you wish to copy and the `of` part is where you wish to paste it, with `/dev/sdb1` being the path to the device you found in step 2.

 If you require further assistance for formatting or creating your image from a Linux computer, check out Intel's official guide at `https://software.intel.com/en-us/programming-blank-sd-card-with-yocto-linux-image-linux`.

- **Windows**: On a Windows platform, refer to the following steps to extract and build an image:

    1. Extract the file using either 7-Zip (`http://www.7-zip.org/`) or WinRAR (`http://www.win-rar.com/`).

    2. Install the Win32 Disk Imager (`http://sourceforge.net/projects/win32diskimager/`). Insert your SD card in the card reader and open it. You may need to run it as an administrator.

       In the app, add the path to the extracted file by clicking on the folder icon. By default, Win32 Disk Imager will only list **Disk Images (*.img, *.IMG)** files. You'll need to click on it and select ***.*** to be able to see all the files. Then, select the file you just extracted and click on **Open**. Now, select the SD card drive name and click on the **Write** button.

 If you require further assistance for formatting or creating your image from a Windows computer, check out Intel's official guide at `https://software.intel.com/en-us/programming-blank-sd-card-with-yocto-linux-image-windows`.

- **Mac OS**: On a Mac OS, go through the following steps to extract and build an image:

    1. Double click on the downloaded file and extract the image file.

    2. Insert your SD card in the card reader and find its system path by using the `diskutil list` command. If you are not sure which one it is, execute the command with and without the SD card inserted in the reader and take note of the line that doesn't repeat in the result of both the commands (for example, `/dev/disk1`).

3. Unmount the SD card by using the `diskutil unmountDisk disk1` command, where `disk1` is your SD card path.

4. Finally, copy the image to the SD card with the `sudo dd if=iot-devkit-latest-mmcblkp0.direct of=/dev/disk1` command. The `if` part of the command is the path to the target image you wish to copy and the `of` part is where you wish to paste it, with `/dev/disk1` being the path to the device you found in step 2. When it finishes, execute the `diskutil eject disk1` command to eject your card, replacing `disk1` with your own device once more.

 If you require further assistance for formatting or creating your image using Mac OS X, check out Intel's official guide at `https://software.intel.com/en-us/programming-blank-sd-card-with-yocto-linux-image-os-x`.

Booting from the IoT Developer Kit image

Now that you have your Developer Kit image, insert it in the Galileo SD card reader and connect it to the Internet by using an Ethernet cable. Power your board on and wait for it to start from the bootable card.

Now, we need to find the Galileo's IP address. Like the Clanton image, this one can also be used with the Arduino IDE. To find your IP address, you can use the Arduino sketch used in the *Finding your board IP address* section in *Chapter 3, Monitoring the Board Temperature*. Upload the sketch using the Arduino IDE and find the IP address printed in the serial monitor. Now, let's access the board from your computer. If you are using Mac OS or Linux, you can execute the `ssh root@my_galileo_ip_address` command from a terminal. In Windows, you should use PuTTY, select the option SSH, and in the **Host Name (or IP address)** field, type `root@my_galileo_ip_address`. Replace `my_galileo_ip_address` with the one your board is using.

If everything went right, you should now see the shell displaying the following command line:

```
root@galileo:~#
```

Check the image version by executing this command:

```
cat /etc/version
```

Checking the IoT Developer Kit image version

Your version doesn't need to be exactly the same as the preceding one. As long as it is a more recent version, it should work fine.

Setting up the Wi-Fi access

As mentioned earlier, all the projects we will be developing can use either a wired or wireless connection to access the Internet. To use a wireless connection from Linux, we'll have to do some configurations. With your board powered off, attach your Wi-Fi adapter just like we did it in the *Connecting through Wi-Fi* section in *Chapter 3, Monitoring the Board Temperature*. Power your Galileo on with the Ethernet cable attached and access it through SSH just like the we did it in the preceding section.

In the SSH shell, type `lspci -k | grep -A 3 -i "network"`. Your Wi-Fi adapter should be printed, as shown in the following screenshot:

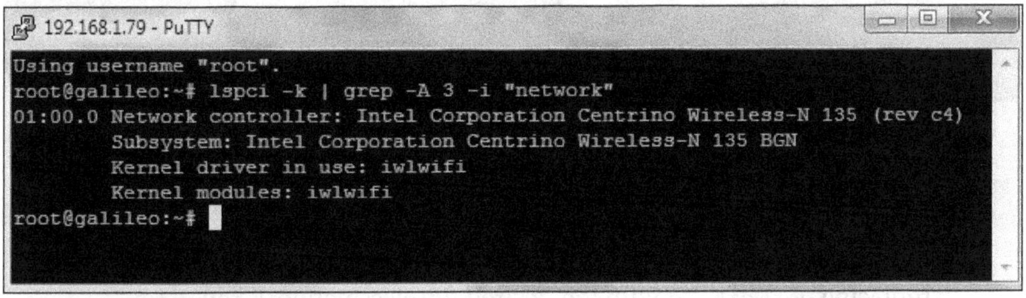

Intel® Centrino Wireless-N 135 was found

If your board doesn't appear printed, you'll need to install its drivers.

This image is installed with the embedded connection manager **connman**, allowing you to easily set up your wireless connection. In the SSH shell, type in the `connmanctl` command and follow these steps:

1. Type `enable wifi` to activate your Wi-Fi adapter. The successful response to this instruction should print in the Wi-Fi enabled shell. If you type `technologies`, you'll be able to see the Wi-Fi connection displayed:

```
192.168.1.79 - PuTTY
connmanctl> technologies
/net/connman/technology/ethernet
  Name = Wired
  Type = ethernet
  Powered = True
  Connected = True
  Tethering = False
/net/connman/technology/wifi
  Name = WiFi
  Type = wifi
  Powered = True
  Connected = False
  Tethering = False
connmanctl>
```

2. Scan the Wi-Fi networks in range by using the `scan wifi` command. To print all the available networks, type `services`. You'll find your wired connection and all the wireless networks in range:

```
192.168.1.79 - PuTTY
connmanctl> services
*AO Wired            ethernet_984fee00050b_cable
   Vodafone-89077D   wifi_0cd292591b86_566f6461666f6e652d383930373744_managed_psk
connmanctl>
```

3. In the previous step, you were able to list the Wi-Fi networks in range. In front of the network SSID, you'll find the network ID. In order to make your board autoconnect to your preferred network, you'll have to execute the `config network_id -autoconnect true -ipv4 dhcp` command, replacing `network_id` with the desired wireless network key.

4. To be able to connect to a secured network, you'll have to enable the connection agent. To do so, type `agent on`, and you'll see **Agent registered** printed.

5. Finally, connect to your selected network by using the `connect network_id` command, where `network_id` is the Wi-Fi network ID (not the SSID). You'll be prompted for your network password.

The MRAA library

Galileo IoT Developer Kit image brings a very useful library named **MRAA**
(https://github.com/intel-iot-devkit/mraa). It is a low-level skeleton for the
I/O communication, helping you stay away from the GPIOs direct manipulation,
which can be harmful if you don't know what you are doing. Like the Arduino
methods to control or read from the board pins, this library offers similar methods,
comprising the following submodules:

- Aio: This contains the methods to read values from the board analog pins
  and change the ADC resolution

- Gpio: This contains the methods to read and write to digital pins

- I2c: This contains the methods to communicate using I2c

- Pwm: This contains the methods to handle the pulse with modulation signals

- Spi: This enables the Spi bus

- Uart: This enables the UART

 If you want to read more about the library's I/O capabilities, visit
https://software.intel.com/en-us/articles/internet-of-
things-using-mraa-to-abstract-platform-io-capabilities.

Let's test this library by reading an analog light sensor. Grab your Grove sensors kit
and connect the light sensor to the Base Shield V2 A0 connector using the 26AWG
Grove cable and attach it to your Galileo board expansion header.

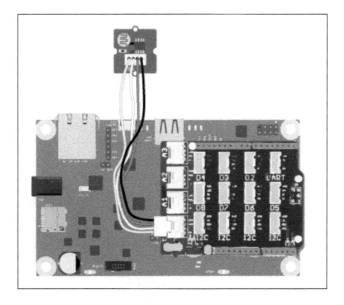

In the Base Shield, you'll find a switch, allowing you to use the shield in 3.3 V or 5 V mode. For this example, make sure it is set to 5 V.

Coming back to the Galileo SSH terminal, let's now create a new folder named `chapter5` to accommodate our test project files. To do so, execute the `mkdir chapter5` command. Enter the directory by typing `cd chapter5`. Since everything in Linux is a file, you'll be able to get a sneak peek into the A0 pin input value by typing `cat ./sys/bus/iio/devices/iio:device0/in_voltage0_raw`. The outputted value should be in the range of 0 to 4095 (12 bit resolution). Although both Intel® Galileo boards provide 12 bit **Analog-to-Digital Converter (ADC)** resolution on the analog pins, when using the MRAA library, the default ADC resolution will be of 10 bits, allowing us to read values in the range of 0 to 1023.

Let's take a look at how we can use this library to read from the light sensor using different development languages.

Node.js

In your Galileo SSH session, create and edit a new file using the vi editor by typing `vi mraaTest.js`. Press *I* to enter the insertion mode and copy and paste the following Node.js script:

```
// Import the library
var m = require('mraa');
console.log('MRAA Version: ' + m.getVersion());

// Export pin A0
var analogPin = new m.Aio(0);

// Read the analog pin raw value
function readValue() {
  var value = analogPin.read();
  console.log(value);
}

// Keep reading from the sensor every second (1000 milliseconds)
setInterval(readValue, 1000);
```

To be able to use the MRAA library in your code, the first thing you need to do is to load it and assign it to a variable by using `var m = require('mraa')`. After exporting the pin A0 with `new Aio(0)`, we are able to start reading the sensor values. Using the `setInterval` method, we are able to keep reading from the sensor by calling the `readValue` method every second. This method reads the input value from the analog pin. You can leave the insertion mode by pressing the *Esc* key. Save the file and leave the editor by typing `:wq`, followed by *Enter*.

Now, let's run the script we just created by executing the `node mraaTest.js` command in the Galileo SSH session. In your terminal, you'll see the raw read values being printed. To stop the script, press *Ctrl* + *C* (or *cmd* + *C* if you are using an Apple keyboard).

The documentation for the MRAA Node.js API can be found at `http://iotdk. intel.com/docs/master/mraa/node/modules/mraa.html`, and taking a look at the **Aio** section, you'll find the `setBit` method, which will allow you to change the ADC bit resolution. If you wish to have more sensibility while reading data from your sensor, you can change the ADC resolution to use 12 bits by adding the line `analogPin.setBit(12)`, after exporting the pin A0. If you run the script again with the same light conditions, you'll see a considerable change in the read values.

Python

Now, let's try doing the same using Python. In your shell, type `vi mraaTest.py`. Type *I* to enter insert mode and copy and paste the following Python code:

```
# Import the MRAA and time libraries
import time
import mraa


print (mraa.getVersion())
# Export the A0 pin
x = mraa.Aio(0)


# Keep reading from sensor every second
while 1:
    print (x.read())
    time.sleep(1)
```

Using `import mraa`, we are able to load the library in our code. To export the analog pin A0, we need to create a `new Aio(0)` object. Having the pin exported, we can read its value by calling the `read` method. Using the `time` library, we can keep reading in loop for every 1 second.

Leave the insertion mode by pressing the *Esc* key. Save the script and leave the editor by typing `:wq`, followed by *Enter*. Now, let's run it by executing the `python mraaTest.py.` command, and you'll have the raw read values printed in the terminal. Changing the incident light will also change the outputted values. To exit the process, press *Ctrl + C* (or *cmd + C*).

 You can find the MRAA Python API documentation at `http://iotdk.intel.com/docs/master/mraa/python/`.

C++

If you prefer, you can just use the C++ library. In your shell, type `vi mraaTest.cpp`. Press *I* to enter the insert mode and copy and paste the following code (`https://github.com/intel-iot-devkit/mraa/blob/master/examples/c%2B%2B/Blink-IO.cpp`):

```
// Import the MRAA library
#include "mraa.hpp"

int main () {
  // Declare vars
  uint16_t adc_value;
  mraa::Aio* a0;

  // Export pin A0
  a0 = new mraa::Aio(0);

  // Keep reading from sensor every second
  while( 1 ) {
    adc_value = a0->read();
    fprintf(stdout, "%d\n", adc_value);
    sleep(1);
  }
}
```

Similar to the previous examples, you'll also have to import the MRAA library to your code and then export the analog pin by creating a new analog pin object on calling `new mraa::Aio(0)`. The `read` method will allow you to obtain the sensor data and when it is used in a `while(1)` loop together with the `sleep` method, it allows us to keep reading the sensor data every second.

Leave the insertion mode by pressing the *Esc* key. Save the script and leave the editor by typing `:wq`, followed by *Enter*. Using C++ , you'll need to compile your code by typing `g++ -std=c++0x mraaTest.cpp -o mytest -lmraa` in to the Galileo terminal. When it finishes compiling, you can run it by executing `./mytest`.

To exit the process, press *Ctrl* + *C* (or *cmd* + *C*).

 As you were able to see, this library provides a great level of abstraction, making it simpler to manipulate the Linux GPIOs. If you wish to have a look at more examples, you can find them at `https://github.com/intel-iot-devkit/mraa/blob/master/examples`.

The UPM library

The UPM (`https://github.com/intel-iot-devkit/upm`) library also comes with the IoT Developer Kit image and acts as a repository for sensors using the MRAA library. With the MRAA library, we were able to read data from the sensor connected to the Galileo analog pin, but the extracted data by itself isn't useful for us. UPM brings a module for Grove sensors, making it possible for us to extract the values that can make sense to us, such as lux values.

While MRAA provides us with low-level methods to read and control the I/O pins, this library makes the development using sensors easier. It supports a list of sensors (`http://iotdk.intel.com/docs/master/upm/modules.html`), making many useful methods available to facilitate controlling or extracting data from them.

Using the circuit that we just used to test MRAA and the Grove sensors UPM library (`libupm-grove`), let's see how we can use the UPM library to obtain lux units from the Light sensors. Inside the `chapter5` folder, create a new file and edit it by typing `viupmTest.js` in the Galileo SSH terminal. Copy and paste the following example (`https://github.com/intel-iot-devkit/upm/blob/master/examples/javascript/grovelight.js`) and let's take a look at it:

```
// Load JavaScript UPM Grove module
var groveSensor = require('jsupm_grove');

// Create the light sensor object using Analog IO pin 0
```

```
var light = new groveSensor.GroveLight(0);

// Read the input and print the raw value and a rough lux value
function readLightSensorValue() {
    console.log(light.name() + " raw value is " + light.raw_value() +
        ", which is roughly " + light.value() + " lux");
}
// Repeat the readLightSensorValue method every second
setInterval(readLightSensorValue, 1000);
```

To have a list of all the sensors available and find the right library to use, we'll have to check the Node.js UPM library documentation, which is available at `http://iotdk.intel.com/docs/master/upm/node/`. In the **APIs** section, you'll find listed all the supported sensors. Expanding the **other** tab, you'll find listed the `grove` module. This module contains the Grove sensors APIs documentation. Clicking on `GroveLight` will display the documentation for the sensor we are using.

To be able to use this library, we need to load the `grove` module first by requiring it with `require('jsupm_grove')`. With the module loaded, we need to create a new Grove sensor that has the subtype `GroveLight` and using the pin A0. Now, we can use the sensor methods:

- `name`: This returns the sensor name
- `raw_value`: This returns the pin's raw read value
- `value`: This returns the read value converted in to lux units

Creating a read interval of 1 second, we'll be printing the name, the raw read value, and the correspondent lux value in loop.

Leave the insertion mode by pressing the *Esc* key. Save the script and leave the editor by typing :*wq*, followed by *Enter*. Run the script on Galileo by typing `node upmTest.js` and you should now see something similar to this printed in the terminal:

Light Sensor raw value is 209, which is roughly 2 lux

Stop the process by pressing *Ctrl + C* (or *cmd + C*).

Like MRAA, you can also use this library in other programming languages:

- **Python**: You can find the Python UPM modules documentation at `http://iotdk.intel.com/docs/master/upm/python`. If you want to try the Python GroveLight demo, you can use the example provided at `https://github.com/intel-iot-devkit/upm/blob/master/examples/python/grovelight.py`. You'll be able to run it using the command `python grovelight.py` in the Galileo terminal.

- **C++**: The C++ UPM modules documentation can be found at `http://iotdk.intel.com/docs/master/upm/modules.html`. If you want to try the C++ GroveLight demo, use the example provided at `https://github.com/intel-iot-devkit/upm/blob/master/examples/c%2B%2B/grovelight.cxx`. You'll be able to compile it using the instruction `g++ -std=c++0x grovelight.cxx -o grovelight -lupm-grove -I /usr/include/upm`. To run, execute the `./grovelight` command in the Galileo terminal.

Summary

As an alternative to developing using the Arduino IDE, there are many more IDEs and tools that are ready to work with Galileo and that will make your life as a developer much easier. Intel® IoT Developer Kit packs a hardware and software solution, allowing you to use other programming languages such as Python or Node.js in your Galileo boards. In this chapter, you had an overview of the IoT Developer Kit components and its concept. You created the Developer Kit bootable image, which we will use in the following chapters and learn how to to use the UPM and MRAA libraries by creating a simple demo to extract data from a Grove light sensor using different programming languages.

In the next chapter, we'll be using this image tools and libraries to build a small meteorological station.

Building an Irrigation System

6

Now that you have your Intel® IoT Developer Kit image built and ready to be used, let's start building some more interesting projects.

One of the fields which is expected to suffer a great and positive impact with IoT is the farming industry. With the rise of the world's population and therefore, the greater food demands, farmers will have to search for new methods to increase their productivity. The Internet of Things can bring more precision and input to help automate all the agricultural operations. It can optimize the crop yields by providing real-time data, allowing farmers to easily identify issues in the fields at an early stage. In between many more applications, it can help them with pest control or even assist in the plantation growing process with automated systems such as irrigation.

In this context, you'll learn how to use sensor's inputs to help you in monitoring and watering your own house plants. We'll start by building a real-time chart using **Wyliodrin** to help you understand how temperature, light, and soil moisture sensors react to environmental changes. Then we'll harvest the sensors' data inputs and send them to the Intel IoT cloud-based analytics system, where we'll monitor them and create watering actuation rules based on the collected data.

In this chapter, you'll learn:

- Setting up your SD card image to enable Wyliodrin
- Reading data from sensor using Wyliodrin's visual programming
- Using Wyliodrin to create a real-time sensorial data chart over time
- Collecting and sending sensors' data to a cloud-based analytics system
- Using Intel® IoT cloud analytics to define actuation rules based on the collected data
- Implementing an actuation behavior

Required component

To be able to complete all the chapter steps, besides the Galileo board, breadboard, and, wires, we'll use some of the sensors contained in the Grove Starter Kit, plus – Intel IoT edition. We'll also use a generic analog soil moisture sensor that is not contained in the mentioned kit:

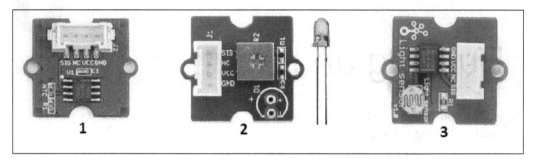

Grove sensors used in the project

We'll be using a Grove LED, Grove Temperature, and Grove Light sensors. These sensors are there in the Grove starter kit plus – Intel IoT edition. To be able to connect the sensors to your board, you'll need to use the Grove Base Shield V2 and the 26AWG Grove cables contained in this kit. If you prefer, you can use other type of sensors, but if they don't have a UPM module available (http://iotdk.intel.com/docs/master/upm/modules.html), you'll only be able to use them with the MRAA library. Let's take a look at these Grove sensors:

- **Grove Temperature**: The Grove temperature sensor is a thermistor-based sensor. It is an analog sensor that allows us to obtain the ambient temperature.

- **Grove LED**: The Grove LED sensor is an LED circuit already using a protective resistor. You can use a different LED (also included in the kit) of multiple colors with this circuit. You'll have to connect an LED to the sensor base circuit. Remember that the longer lead should be connected to the + side of the connector, and the shorter lead to the - side. We'll be using this module to simulate a sprinkler or water pump and be able to have a visual feedback about its status.

- **Grove Light**: This is the sensor we used in the previous chapter to test the libraries. As you were able to see, it is light sensitive.

- **Besides the Grove sensors**: We'll also use an FC-28 Soil Moisture sensor (`http://www.ebay.com/itm/Soil-Humidity-Moisture-Detection-Sensor-Module-Arduino-w-Dupont-Wires-kits-SWTG-/231560321363`). It is an interesting sensor that allows us to get some valuable information when there's a soil water shortage or the opposite. This is how an FC-28 Soil Moisture sensor looks:

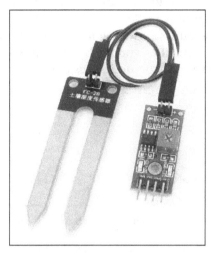

An FC-28 soil moisture sensor.

You can use any sensor of this kind, as long as it accepts an input voltage of 5 V. This one in specific has a digital and an analog output, providing us a low and a high level, or a more precise output using analog values. These sensor resistance values will decrease when the water exposure increases.

Setting up Wyliodrin

Working with the vi editor in a Galileo's shell can be very stressful if you are beginning with Linux development, and want to check how your sensors work.

In this chapter, we'll have a closer look at the Wyliodrin development tool and what it can offer us. It is an online editor that makes it possible to build our applications just by dragging, dropping, and attaching components, just like Legos. It can also be used just as a simple editor for Python or JavaScript code. All the code is developed using its website, and it will be pushed to Galileo when you want to run it. Another great feature is that it allows you to build customizable dashboards and charts fed by your own data signals. This development tool is not entirely free, but you can use most of its resources with a nonpaying account. It is a really nice tool to help you debug and understand how your sensors work.

Let's set up our image to allow Wyliodrin to connect to it:

1. Open Wyliodrin's website (`https://www.wyliodrin.com/`) in your computer's browser, and sign in with your preferred account. You can use your Facebook, Google, or GitHub account. As soon as you sign in, see your dashboard; all the projects you create will be listed there.

2. The next thing to do should be adding your Galileo board to your account. In the top-left corner of your dashboard page, locate the **Add new board** button. Click on the button, and you'll be asked to name and identify your board. Feel free to name it as you wish, but in the **Gadget:** selection box, select **Intel Galileo**. Once you do it, press the **Next** button:

Identifying your board

3. At this step, you can set up your board's Wi-Fi connection. If you prefer using Wi-Fi, check the **Use Wireless** box and fill in your network details. If you just use a cabled connection, press the **Submit** button. All the following steps will now be displayed on your screen. Following those guidelines, you'll need to insert the SD card, containing the Intel IoT Developer Kit image, in a computer with an SD card reader. If you didn't create the image in the previous chapter, you'll have to do it now. Close the modal window by clicking on any place outside it.

4. Close to the **Add new board** button, you'll find the board you just added, listed. There should also be a sprocket symbol. Click on it and select the option **Download wyliodrin.json**. Your board configuration file will be downloaded:

Downloading wyliodrin.json file

5. With the SD card in your computer's card reader, paste the downloaded file to its root directory, having the exact name, that is, `wyliodrin.json`:

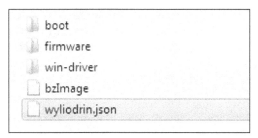

Paste the downloaded file in the root of the SD card

6. Eject the SD card from your computer and place it in your Galileo. Connect the Ethernet cable (if not using Wi-Fi) and plug it in. Wait a couple of seconds, and in your dashboard, you'll see your board status appearing as **Online**:

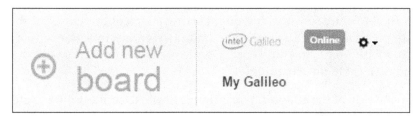

Board successfully detected

Now you are ready to start developing your apps using Wyliodrin.

 If you are having troubles activating your board, you can find the official tutorial at `https://www.wyliodrin.com/wiki/boards_setup/arduinogalileo`.

Using Wyliodrin to read from the sensors

Now that your Galileo is connected to your Wyliodrin account, let's understand how to use it to extract data from our sensors. We'll be using the Visual programming language to print the raw read values to our console and use them to create a real-time chart with all the sensors' inputs.

Let's start by wiring the circuit.

Wiring the sensors

Using the Grove sensors, you'll need to attach the Grove Base Shield V2 to the Galileo expansion header. This type of sensor has its own 26AWG Grove cables. With Galileo's power off, and using the Grove cables, connect the Grove Temperature sensor to the shield A0 connector, the Grove Light sensor to the A1 connector, and the Grove LED to the D8 connector.

> If you prefer using other sensors that aren't part of the Grove kit, you'll be able to use them as long as they can work with 5 V. Connect them to the Galileo Arduino expansion header pins using the same pins that the Grove sensors are using. For the LED, you can use digital pin 8 as well, but remember to add a protective resistor (1 KΩ should be fine) to its circuit, just like we used earlier in in the *Fading an LED* subsection under the *Running your first sketches* section in *Chapter 2, Rediscovering the Arduino IDE*.

Now, only the Moisture sensor is missing. Having a look at the sensor, it should bring an adapter. On one of its sides, you'll find two connectors, one with a + sign and the other with – sign. In your sensor, locate the two connectors with the + and – signs, and connect them accordingly.

In the opposite side of the adapter, you'll find four pins. Connect the adapter VCC pin to Galileo's 5 V pin and the adapter GND pin to the Galileo's ground pin. The two remaining pins allow you to obtain both digital and analog value readings. Connect the adapter analog connector A0 to Galileo's analog pin A2. The remaining adapter pin A0 won't be used, but it lets you read a value 1 when the read values are above a threshold or 0 when they are below. The threshold can be adjusted using the adapter potentiometer. The following figure shows how the circuit should look:

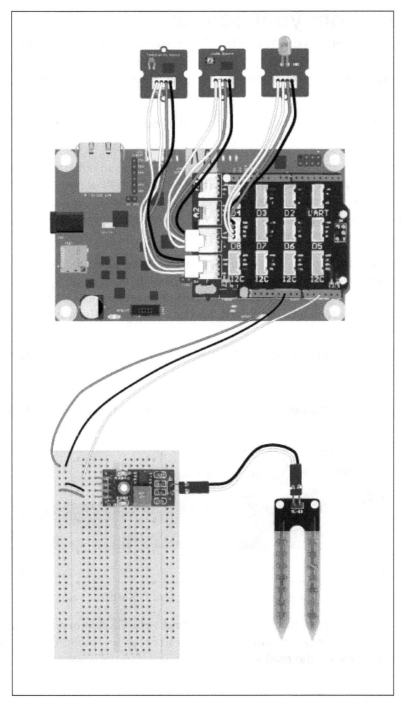

Wiring the sensors

Reading from your sensors

Back to your browser, in your Wyliodrin dashboard, click on **Create new application** to create a new app. Fill in your application title and as language, select **New project – Visual programming**. In the next step, you can press the **Submit** button, since we won't use any extra components.

Now in the editor, let's start by reading from the Moisture sensor, which is connected to the analog pin A2.

Similar to the previous examples, we need to have a loop to help us keep reading periodically. On the left-hand side of the project, click on **Program**, then on **Loops**, and finally, on the first option, **Repeat every 1 seconds do**. Drag the block and position it anywhere in your sketch. This will be the main loop cycle we'll be using to extract the sensor's data every second.

To read from the analog pin, we can use an **analogRead** block located inside the **Pin Access** selector. Set the pin number to 2 so that we can read from A2. To be able to output the read values, you should add a **Print on screen** block ,which can be found inside **Program | Screen and keyboard**, and put the **analogRead** block inside.

 You can find the Visual language documentation at https://www.wyliodrin.com/wiki/languages/visual.

Put both the print blocks inside the loop block to keep reading and printing every second.

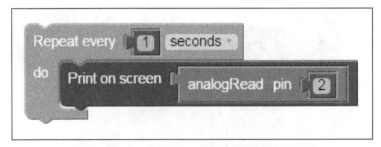

Visual programming blocks to print read data in the console

On the left-hand side of your window, you'll find your Galileo in a list, with the title **Run application on**. Click on your board name in order to upload the code, and you should now be noticing the read values being printed in the app console.

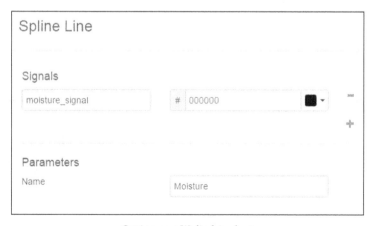

```
255
Moisture Sensor
255
Moisture Sensor
255
Moisture Sensor
255
Moisture Sensor
255
Moisture Sensor
255
```

Printing read values from the Moisture sensor

Taking a look at the Visual programming **analogRead** block documentation (`https://www.wyliodrin.com/wiki/languages/visual#analog_read`), you'll find that this block maps the read values between 0 and 255. To stop running the code in Galileo, press the **Stop** button and close the modal window by clicking on the close symbol.

Now, instead of outputting the read values to the console, let's try outputting them as a signal to Wyliodrin. This service allow us to create real-time charts that can be fed straight from our sensors. Click on the **Dashboard** link located in the top-right corner of the window, and let's give it a try.

On the right-hand side of the window, you'll find many chart types listed. Scroll down a bit and add a **Spline Line** chart. Click on the chart settings button (sprocket icon), name the signal `moisture_signal` and the chart as `Moisture`.

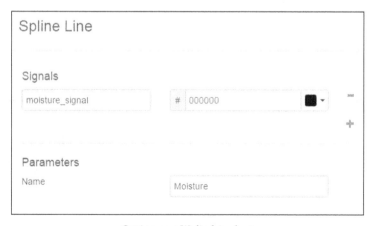

Setting up a Wyliodrin chart

Click on the **X** button to save and exit.

Getting back to the editor by clicking the **Dashboard** link again, let's now emit signals with the read values to fill the chart we have just created inside the section **Signals**; you'll find the **Send signal with value** block, which can be used to send data to the chart. Replace the print block with this one and replace the value with the **analogRead** block, as shown in the following figure:

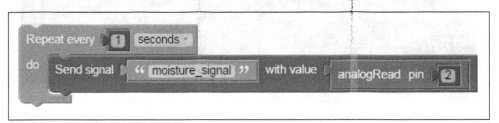

Visual programming blocks to feed a chart with the sensor data

This way, we'll be sending the read data straight to the chart, feeding it every second. Running your application again, you'll see the chart being filled with the read data over time.

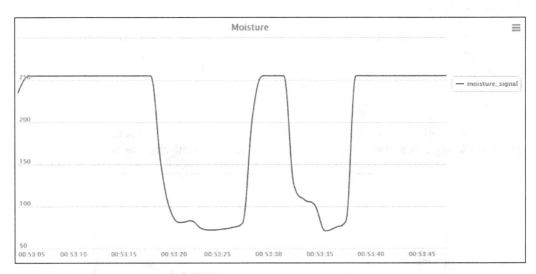

Soil Moisture sensor response to water

Use a glass of water and wet your Moisture sensor a bit. You'll see the chart values decreasing. The more amount of water you apply to this type of sensor, the more conductive it will be. Its resistivity values are higher when it is dry. The values displayed in the chart refer to the read voltage values at Galileo's analog pin, mapped from 0 to 255. Reading a value of 255 means we are receiving 5 V at the Galileo pin.

So far, we were able to read from the Soil Moisture sensor. Now, let's add the remaining sensors to our real-time chart:

1. Create two more **Send signal** blocks and place them inside the loop.
2. Add one **analogRead** to each of the new **Send signal** blocks in the value field.
3. Name the temperature signal as temperature_signal and set the **analogRead** block pin as 0.
4. Name the light signal as light_signal and set the **analogRead** block pin as 1.

Now you should be able to send all the sensors' values to the Wyliodrin charts, and your blocks should look similar to this:

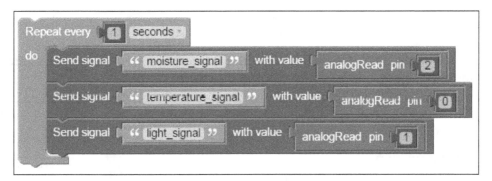

Sending all sensors data to charts

Click on the **Dashboard** button and let's add the new signals to the chart. Edit the **Spline Line** chart and click on the **+** button to add the remaining sensors. Give each of the line a color to help you in identifying them and name your chart as well.

Adding more signals to the chart

Now you'll be able to plot the line chart with the three sensors' data and in real time. Run the applications, and let's take a look at the chart:

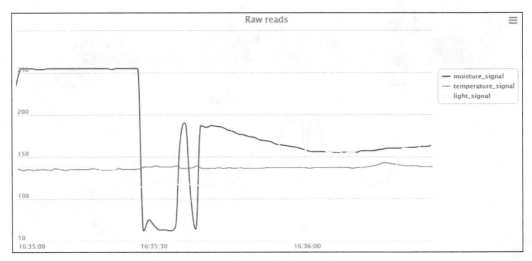

Sensors behaviour

If you are using the same signal colors, you should have the raw soil moisture values in black, the raw light values in yellow, and the raw temperature values in red. Expose your Light sensor to more or less light, and observe the changes in the real-time chart. If you heat or try placing the temperature sensor in another place, you'll most likely find different values being plotted as well.

You'll notice that the temperature and light sensors' values will increase when the temperature and incident light increase, while the Moisture sensor will have a different behavior with the printed values decreasing when water is applied to it.

Controlling an irrigation system using sensorial data

Now that we are able to understand the sensors' behavior, let's use them to help us creating a lawn watering system. To help us on our task, we'll be using the Intel IoT cloud-based analytics. This is a free service for developers, allowing real-time data acquisition and analysis. We'll be able to collect our sensors' data, analyze it, and create actuation rules based on the given inputs.

To simulate the irrigation system working, we'll be recurring to an LED. We won't be controlling a real irrigation system, but with these instructions, you'll be able to easily adapt this example to a real life situation.

Making your sensor data available online

Let's start by taking a look at the enableiot website and create a user account:

1. Open the `https://dashboard.us.enableiot.com/` link with your favorite browser and create an account by providing your e-mail and password.

2. Go to your e-mail inbox and look for the e-mail Intel just sent you. Follow the included link to finish creating your account, and you'll be asked to add an account name. Give your account a name to finish the registration process.

By the end of the account creation process, you should be seeing the analytics dashboard displaying the account global status, and with no registered devices.

To communicate with the analytics servers and to be able to exchange data with your Galileo board, you have two main options available:

- **REST API**: This allows us to communicate directly with the Intel® cloud using the HTTP protocol. It can be used for sending or requesting data on behalf of a specific account and device. You can read more about it at `https://github.com/enableiot/iotkit-api/wiki/Api-Home`.

- **iotkit-agent**: This is comprised of the iotkit-admin and iotkit-agent. The first one is a command-line wrapper for some useful REST API requests, while the iotkit-agent is an agent that runs as a daemon in your Galileo. It allows us to locally communicate with it, using TCP or UDP packets and by its turn, the agent itself, will also communicate with the analytics servers in your behalf. To read more about it, refer to `https://github.com/enableiot/iotkit-agent`.

Since the IoT Developer Kit image already brings the iotkit-agent installed and running as a daemon, we'll be using it to communicate with the analytics servers.

Make sure your board has Internet access, and the IoT Developer Kit bootable image in the Galileo SD card reader. Connect to it through SSH and check whether your system date is correct by typing the `date` command. If the date is not right, set the right one using `date -s "YYYY-MM-DD HH:MM:SS"`, replacing `YYYY` with the year, `MM` with the month, `DD` with the day, `HH` with the hour, `MM` with the minutes, and `SS` with the seconds:

1. Also, make sure you are using the latest iotkit-agent version running the following command:

    ```
    root@galileo:~# npm update -g iotkit-agent
    ```

2. The update process will take several minutes to conclude. Once it finishes, you can check whether the agent is able to connect with analytics servers by executing the following command:

    ```
    root@galileo:~# iotkit-admin test
    ```

3. The command will produce the following output, confirming that not only the agent is running, but that it was also able to reach and connect with the analytics servers:

```
root@galileo:~# iotkit-admin test
2015-06-24T00:10:54.285Z - info: Trying to connect to host ...
2015-06-24T00:10:56.505Z - info: Connected to dashboard.us.enableiot.com
2015-06-24T00:10:56.522Z - info: Environment: prod
2015-06-24T00:10:56.528Z - info: Build: 0.14.1
root@galileo:~#
```

Testing agent's connectivity

If you are connecting behind a firewall with a proxy, you may need to add the configuration to your agent, using the `iotkit-admin proxy «proxy server» «proxy port»` command.

The next step is activating our Galileo device:

1. In the analytics website, visit the account section by clicking on the menu icon located in the top-left side of the web page and then on the **Account** option.

2. In this section, you'll be able to generate an **Activation Code** by clicking on the renew icon. Each time you generate one, it will only be valid for an hour. If you let the code expire without activating your board, you'll have to generate a new one.

3. Click on the eye icon to see the activation code and copy it.

4. To ensure that you have a clean environment, in the SSH shell, type the `iotkit-admin initialize` command.

5. Finally, to activate the board, run the `iotkit-admin activate «activation_code»` command, replacing «activation_code» with the generated code.

You can confirm that everything went right by checking the **Devices** section in the analytics website. The device you had just activated should appear listed. Clicking on its **Id** will show you all the details and allow you to make some changes, such as in the board name.

With the device activated, we should now register our components. Components can be sensors with observations over time or actuators that can be remotely controlled.

Once again, navigate to the analytics website **Account** section, but now click on the **Catalog** separator. You'll find three default component types displayed: **Temperature**, **Humidity**, and **Power**. These types are used to identify and group sensors/actuators with the common properties.

The Grove Temperature sensor and Grove LED actuator can respectively match with the **temperature.v1.0** and **powerswitch.v1.0** existing types, but the Light sensor and the Moisture sensor will need new component types.

For the Light sensor, we'll have to create a new type. Click on **Add new Catalog Item** and fill in the following information to create the light type:

Component Name	Type	Data Type	Format	Unit of measure	Display
light	Sensor	Number	Integer	lux	Time Series

For the Soil Moisture sensor, we can create a new version of the existing **Humidity** type. Click on the listed **humidity.v1.0** component type and then on **New Version**. Fill in the form with the following information:

Type	Data Type	Format	Unit of measure	Display
Sensor	Number	Integer	Raw ADC value	Time Series

To be able to register our components with these new types in the agent, we'll have to restart it using the following command:

```
root@galileo:~# systemctl restart iotkit-agent
```

Now, let's register our sensors and actuators by executing the following commands in the SSH shell:

- `iotkit-admin register grove-temperature temperature.v1.0`: This command will register the Temperature sensor with the type temperature.v1.0

- `iotkit-admin register sprinkler powerswitch.v1.0`: This command will register the LED actuator with the name `sprinkler` and type `powerswitch.v1.0`

- `iotkit-admin register grove-light light.v1.0`: This command will register the Grove Light sensor with the new type `light`

- `iotkit-admin register moisture-sensor humidity.v1.1`: This command will register the Moisture Sensor with the new version of `humidity` type

To confirm that all the components were registered successfully, in the SSH shell, type the following command:

```
root@galileo:~# iotkit-admin components
```

All the registered components will be displayed in the terminal:

```
root@galileo:~# iotkit-admin components

id : t              Name                cID

temperature.v1.0    grove-temperature

powerswitch.v1.0    sprinkler

light.v1.0          grove-light

humidity.v1.1       moisture-sensor
```

Registered components

Now we are ready to start sending data to the analytics cloud.

Download this chapter's source code from the Packt website. You can download it straight to your board using the command `wget «code_url»` and then extract the compressed files using **Unzip**. Use the command `unzip «compressed_filename».zip` to extract its contents. Inside the **_3_Collecting_data** folder, you'll find the `index.js` file. Let's take a look at it.

In this file, we are using UDP packets to communicate with the local agent. The agent will be listening on port `41234`.

The first thing we need to do is to initialize our sensors:

```
var temperatureSensor = new upm.GroveTemp(0);
var lightSensor = new upm.GroveLight(1);
var moistureSensor = new mraa.Aio(2);
var sprinkler = new upm.GroveLed(8);
```

For the Grove sensors and actuators, we are able to use the UPM Grove library to extract lux and temperature units, or have available methods to control the Grove LED. The Moisture sensor doesn't have a UPM module available, and we'll have to extract its value using the MRAA lib.

To help us writing our sensors observations, we had created a method named `sendObservation`, accepting a sensor identification and the read value. This method will send a UDP packet to the local agent, making him/her send the observation to the analytics servers:

```
function sendObservation(name, value){
  var msg = JSON.stringify({
    n: name,
    v: value
  });

  var sentMsg = new Buffer(msg);
  console.log("Sending observation: " + sentMsg);
  client.send(sentMsg, 0, sentMsg.length, options.client.port,
options.client.host);
};
```

To keep extracting and sending our sensors' data to the agent, we use a `setInterval` loop, repeating the whole process every five seconds:

```
setInterval(function () {
  sendObservation('grove-temperature', temperatureSensor.value());
  sendObservation('grove-light', lightSensor.value());
  sendObservation('moisture-sensor', moistureSensor.read());
}, 5000);
```

Make sure the iotkit-agent is running using the `systemctl status iotkit-agent` command. Look at the command output, and if the service is not tagged as **Active (running)**, you'll have to start it by running the `systemctl start iotkit-agent` command. Now let's see what this code will really produce. Run it with the `node index.js` command, and you'll be able to see in the terminal the values that are being sent to the agent.

Open the Intel analytics website and in the menu, select the **Charts** option. Tick your device and then the **All** tick box inside the **Component** section so that you can watch all the sensors' data being used to build a chart. Click on the refresh button and change the chart refresh date to **5 seconds**. Wait a bit, and you'll see the chart being drawn:

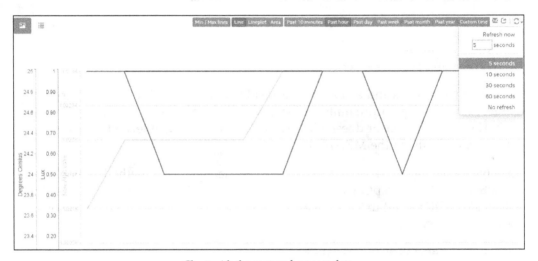

Chart with the captured sensors data

Every five seconds, the chart will be updated with the new sensors' measurements. You'll have a specific scale for each metric. If you are not able to see any data in the chart, check the agent logs with the `tail -f /tmp/agent.log` command. If you are not able to access the log file, it is possible that your agent is not running.

Now that we have our data available online, let's now learn how to use it to control the sprinkler.

Creating rules for actuation

The iotkit-agent not only is capable of sending data online, but is also capable of doing actuation requests for our board. To be able to receive this type of request, our Galileo agent must be using the MQTT protocol when communicating with the analytics servers. In the Galileo SSH session, type `iotkit-admin protocol mqtt` to ensure that the agent is using it.

When an action is triggered, the analytics cloud will send a MQTT message to the Galileo agent. The agent will then send a UDP packet to the localhost port 41235.

Edit the index.js file located inside the downloaded folder _4_Collecting_and_ actuating. If you notice, this piece of code contains the code used in the previous example for data collection, but now is also listening to UDP connections on port 41235:

```
server.on("message", function (msg, rinfo) {
   console.log("server got: " + msg + " from " +
rinfo.address + ":" + rinfo.port

   // Ignore messages unless they are local
   if(rinfo.address != "127.0.0.1") return;

   var js = JSON.parse(msg);
   var component = js.component;
   var command = js.command;
   var argvArray = js.argv;

   // Ignore requests that are not for sprinkler actions
   if (component !== 'sprinkler') return;

   for(var i = 0; i < argvArray.length; i++) {
     var name = argvArray[i].name;
     var value = argvArray[i].value;
       if (value === '1') {
            sprinkler.on();
         setTimeout(function () {
           sprinkler.off();
         }, 5000);
     }
         if (value === '0') sprinkler.off();
   }
});
```

Whenever a valid actuation message arrives, we'll check whether it is a sprinkler component. The target values will be contained inside the argvArray array variable. Whenever we receive a value of 1, we will turn the sprinkler (LED) on for 5 seconds. If we receive the value 0, the sprinkler will turn off. Run this code using the node index.js command.

In the analytics website menu, select the option **Control**. Here, we are able to define the commands that will be sent to our board's agent. Select your device and the sprinkler component by ticking the respective check boxes. Now in the **Add action** section, select **Led(0,1)** as the **Parameter name**, select the value **1** for the **Parameter value**, and select mqtt as **Transport Type**. Click on the **Add action** button and then on **Save as complex command** to save this request. Name the actuation command as Turn sprinkler ON. The saved request will appear at the top of the web page inside the **Complex commands** section. In this section, click on the command you just created, scroll to the bottom of the page, and press **Send**. If everything went right, your LED should now be turned on, confirming that you were able to control it from the Internet.

Now, let's create a new complex command to turn the sprinkler (LED) off. Once again, head to the **Add action** section and repeat the steps we used to create the previous complex command, this time setting the **Parameter value** as 0. Add the action and save the complex command as Turn sprinkler OFF. Like earlier, a new button will appear at the top of the page, referring the new command. Click on it and then on **Send** to turn the LED off.

At this point, we are able to collect sensors' data and control our sprinkler remotely. Now, let's create a rule triggered by the collected data that will be able to control the sprinkler:

1. In the analytics website menu, click on the **Rules** option and then on the **Add a rule** button.

   The first form will let you configure the rule details. Give your rule a suggestible name like Start irrigation by filling the **Rule Name** text field and select a **Priority** level. In the **Notifications type** selection area, depending on the selected notification type, you'll be able to receive an e-mail and an actuation request or have a specific URL being called when the rule is triggered. Select the **Email** option to add it and select your e-mail from the selection list. Click again on the **Notifications type** selection list and now select the **Actuation** option. On the right-hand side of the page, a new form will appear, allowing you to select the actuation command. Select the Turn sprinkler ON command.

   Click on **Next** to move to the **Devices** form.

2. In this new screen, you'll be able to select the board you want to use. Since you should only have one being displayed, tick your device checkbox to select it from the list and click on **Next**.

3. Now at the **Conditions** step, we can define our rule triggers. Let's add some basic conditions so that we can test triggering the action.

    In the **Monitored Measure** section, we can select the sensor we want to use in the rule. Select the **grove-light** monitored measure, and taking a look at the sensors charts, we can observe that the current lux value for this room is of 1 lux. Set the trigger condition to use the basic condition **>= 1**. This will make the rule trigger when the analytics servers receive a light value above 1 lux. Now, let's add two more conditions for the remaining sensors. Click on the **+** button located in the top-right corner of the web page to get more conditions and in the **Add conditions** select box, select the option **All conditions are satisfied** to create an intersection rule with the new condition.

    Select the **grove-temperature** sensor and add the basic condition between, setting the values 0 to 40. Click again on the **+** sign to add a condition for the Soil Moisture sensor. Select the sensor and add the basic condition **<= 500**.

    Ticking the **Enable Automatic Reset** checkbox will allow this rule to be triggered again without acknowledging the received notification. Tick this box and click on the **Done** button when you finish it.

Now, let's test it. In your Galileo SSH terminal, navigate to the `_4_Collecting_and_actuating` folder and run the code with the `node index.js` command. To be able to trigger the rule you just created, you'll have to be in the 0 – 40 degree Celsius temperature range, have more luminosity than 1 lux, and must have the moisture sensor wet. Try to bring these three conditions together, and after about half a minute, the actuation request will arrive in your board, turning the sprinkler (LED) on. You'll be able to read the message in the console. The sprinkler will be on for 10 seconds, and then Galileo will turn it off. Since we've also defined the e-mail actuation in the rule, if you open your e-mail, you'll have a new notification from the Intel IoT analytics website.

A quick Internet research about how you should irrigate certain types of plants will help you create rules for a real system. For instance, grass usually is irrigated at dawn and noon (light sensor), and when the temperature (temperature sensor) is very high, the irrigation cycle is skipped. Also, you won't want to add more water to the plants if they have already enough moisture (Soil Moisture sensor).

Using this rules system, you can not only start the watering process, but also stop it only when certain conditions are gathered.

> This is just a basic example with learning purposes. If you wish to create a real sprinkler system, you'll need to isolate your circuit from water and replace your LED with a relay connected to a water pump.

Summary

In this chapter, you were able to see a simple idea about how IoT can help the agriculture sector. We created a small irrigation system that actuates based on the gathered information from the sensors.

With sensors being a key part of this project, we started by studying them and understanding their behavior with environmental changes. After understanding how the sensors work, we were able to understand what they are able to do in this sector. We've collected data from our sensors and made it online, so that it could be analyzed by a rules system. By defining rules, we were able to trigger the irrigation process.

In the next chapter, we'll have a different topic; we'll create a Christmas animation with light and music.

7
Creating Christmas Light Effects

In the previous chapter, we were able to control an irrigation system based on the gathered sensorial data. In this chapter, we'll create a different type of project. Using a digitally-addressable LED strip and the YouTube IFrame Player API, we'll create our own Christmas lighting animations with music videos and light effects. We'll use the Socket.IO real-time engine to control all the animations from a web page that can be used from a mobile device's web browser. You'll learn how to control an LED strip, create basic light animations, and play music videos along with them.

In this chapter, we'll learn:

- Wiring and controlling an LPD8806 LED strip
- Building simple asynchronous LED animations
- Creating a basic control page
- Using the YouTube IFrame API to control a video playlist
- Coordinating animations using the Socket.IO real-time engine

Required component

For this chapter, we'll also be using the Intel IoT Dev Kit bootable image. Besides the Galileo board and its wiring requirements along with an Internet connection, you'll need to have an LPD8806 LED strip (http://www.adafruit.com/product/306).

The LPD8806 LED strip

This type of LED strip is a digitally-addressable colored strip. It is not a cheap component, but will help you achieve some real, nice colored and glowing effects. Feel free to choose the length of your strip, but note that long strips will require you to use an external 5 V power supply unit. Using a 5 V, 2 Amperes power supply should be enough for powering a 1 m strip (http://www.adafruit.com/products/276).

Wiring the LED strip

The LPD8806 LED strip is a digitally-addressable RGB LED strip that can receive instructions using the SPI protocol. This type of strip is one of the most customizable available as you can control the colors of each of the available LEDs individually using 21 bit colors per LED.

Galileo is great for this task since it has a native SPI controller (only actuates as master) available. This way, you don't need to bit-bang the GPIO pins, simulating the hardware behavior through software, which consumes more CPU usage when compared to the hardware option.

Common serial ports communicate asynchronously since there is no control over data transmission as the same transfer rates are being used. The SPI controller works differently. Being a synchronous data bus, it uses two different lines—one for data and the other for a clock signal. The clock signal will tell the receiver when it should start looking at the transmitted data. This is an interesting protocol since it can be used with simple shift registers, just like our LED strip.

Taking a look at the LED strip, you'll find four wire connectors: **5V**, **GND**, **CI**, and **DI**. Each of these (input) connectors require to have a wire attached to it and you may have to solder them. Visit `https://learn.adafruit.com/digital-led-strip/wiring` if you need help for doing this.

On the opposite side of the strip, you'll find four other connectors, but those ones are used for output and won't be necessary unless you want to add more LEDs to your strip.

Having in mind your strip length, you may need to consider powering it from an external **5V** power source. If you are using a strip containing only a couple of LEDs, you should be able to power it straight from the Galileo's **5V** pin, as displayed in the following figure:

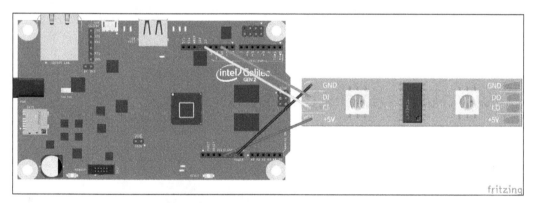

Powering a small LED strip from Galileo

The **DI** connector refers to the data line input and should be connected to Galileo's pin 10, while the **CI** (clock input) connector should be connected to Galileo's pin 13.

If you are using a short strip, connect the **5V** and **GND** strip connectors to the Galileo's **5V** and **GND** pins, respectively. If you are using a longer strip, you should power it from an external **5V** power supply, sharing **Ground** with the Galileo, as displayed in the following figure:

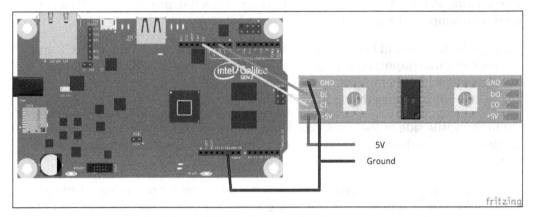

Powering the LED strip from an external power source

 If your board keeps freezing, especially when trying to display the white color, you'll definitely need to use an external power supply unit to power your LED strip.

Controlling the LED strip

Now that we've finished wiring the LED strip to the Galileo board properly, let's see how we can control it by filling it all red.

For this project, we'll be using Node.js and the LPD8806 UPM library.

 You can find the LPD8806 UPM library Node.js documentation at `http://iotdk.intel.com/docs/master/upm/node/classes/lpd8806.html`. Under the **Methods** tab, you'll find all the available methods.

This library uses the MRAA library SPI module (`http://iotdk.intel.com/docs/master/mraa/node/classes/spi.html`) and provides a simple way to interact with the strip, abstracting the SPI writing process. It works by filling an array of pixels with color information and writing it to the SPI bus. You can set up each LED individually using the `setPixelColor(pixelPosition, Red, Green, Blue)` method and actually write to the strip using the `show()` method.

Let's try creating a simple script to make the strip completely red. Connect to your Galileo using SSH and create a new folder named `chapter7`.

Inside the new folder type `vi test.js`, enter the insertion mode using the key *I* and paste the following script:

```
var LPD8806 = require('jsupm_lpd8806').LPD8806;
console.log('Setting all leds red...');


var stripLength = 30;
var chipSelect = 0;


// The second parameter is the CS (chip select).
var ledstrip = new LPD8806(stripLength, chipSelect);


// Set each led full red. Max accepted value per color component is 255
for (var i = 0; i != ledstrip.getStripLength(); ++i) {
  ledstrip.setPixelColor(i, 255, 0, 0);
}


ledstrip.show();
console.log('The strip should now be all red!');
```

Change the `stripLength` variable to the number of LEDs your strip contains and the The `chipSelect` variable can be set to 0 since this type of strip doesn't have a chip select (CS) pin. After initializing the strip by creating a new `LPD8806` object, you can check the strip length using the `getStripLength` method.

To run this piece of code, type in the `node fullRed.js` SSH console. If everything went right, you should now see your strip all colored red. Looping the entire strip and setting the right RGB color, we are able to fill it red. Using the `show` method, we make it all visible.

Creating a real-time server

Now let's create a real-time web server to allow us to control the strip from a web page that can be accessed from any browser. We'll be building two web pages: one to control the strip and another to play YouTube videos from a playlist.

To enable real-time communication, we'll be using the Socket.IO real-time engine. In the SSH shell and inside the project folder, install the Socket.IO Node.js module using the `npm install socket.io` command. The operation will install some dependencies and will take a couple of minutes to conclude.

Socket.IO allows us to exchange real-time messages between our web pages and our server.

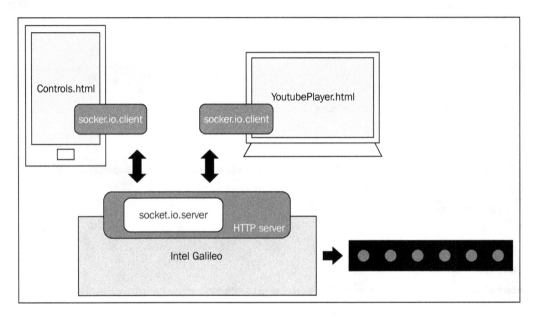

Galileo will run the server, while the browsers will run the clients. Clients will connect to the server and bidirectional communication channels will be established between each of them.

Create a new file, name it `index.js`, and paste the following code:

```js
var fs = require('fs');

var routesViews = {
  '/player': 'youtubePlayer.html',
  '/controls': 'controls.html'
};

var handler = function (request, response) {
  var view = routesViews[request.url];

  if (!view) {
    response.writeHeader(401, {"Content-Type": "text/html"});
```

```
      response.write('Page does not exist');
      response.end();
    } else {

      fs.readFile(view, function (err, html) {
        if (err) {
          throw err;
        }

        response.writeHeader(200, {"Content-Type": "text/html"});
        response.write(html);
        response.end();
      });
    }
  };



  var app = require('http').createServer(handler);
  var io = require('socket.io')(app);

  app.listen(8080);
  console.log('Listening..');
```

As mentioned previously, we'll be serving two pages from two different endpoints. We'll be serving the YouTube player from `/player` and the controls page from `/controls`. Those files will be scripted in separate files, but we'll be loading and serving them from here. To do so, we'll use the filesystem Node.js library `fs`.

 This library is already included with Node.js and doesn't require to be installed separately.

The next thing we are doing is creating an HTTP server and a handler to deal with the incoming requests. The purpose of this handler is to answer the requester with the requested page or with a not found error when the request is unknown. When one of our web pages is requested, the handlers will read the correspondent HTML page from the correspondent HTML file and write it in the response, which will be parsed by the browsers.

For the real-time server, we are assigning our HTTP server to the Socket.IO object and finally, starting to listen for the requests on port `8080`.

Building the control page

Starting with the control page, we'll build it using HTML, jQuery (https://jquery.com/), and also Bootstrap (http://getbootstrap.com/) for a little help on styling.

We'll build a simple page where we will make three buttons available: one for play, one for next, and the last one for stop.

Inside your project folder (chapter7), create the web page using the vi controls.html command and paste the following code:

```html
<!DOCTYPE html>
<html lang="en">
  <head>
    <meta charset="utf-8">
    <meta http-equiv="X-UA-Compatible" content="IE=edge">
    <meta name="viewport" content="width=device-width, initial-scale=1">
    <title>Animation Controls</title>
    <link href="http://maxcdn.bootstrapcdn.com/bootstrap/3.3.4/css/bootstrap.min.css" rel="stylesheet">
    <script src="https://cdnjs.cloudflare.com/ajax/libs/socket.io/1.3.5/socket.io.min.js"></script>
    <script src="https://cdnjs.cloudflare.com/ajax/libs/jquery/2.1.3/jquery.min.js"></script>
  </head>
  <body>
    <script>
      var socket = io('http://192.168.1.79:8080');
    </script>
    <div class="container-fluid" style="text-align: center;">

      <div class="page-header">
        <h1>Animation controls</h1>
      </div>

      <div class="row" style="margin-top: 50px;">

        <div class="col-xs-12" style="margin-top: 30px;">
          <button type="button" class="btn btn-primary btn-lg" data-target-action="play">
            <span class="glyphicon glyphicon-play" aria-hidden="true"></span> Play
          </button>
```

```
        </div>

        <div class="col-xs-12" style="margin-top: 30px;">
          <button type="button" class="btn btn-primary btn-lg" data-
target-action="next">
            <span class="glyphicon glyphicon-step-forward" aria-
hidden="true"></span> Skip
          </button>
        </div>

        <div class="col-xs-12" style="margin-top: 30px;">
          <button type="button" class=""btn btn-danger btn-lg" data-
target-action="stop">
            <span class="glyphicon glyphicon-stop" aria-
hidden="true"></span> Stop
          </button>
        </div>

    </div>
<div class="row" style="bottom:0;position: absolute;">
        Current status
        <span class="badge">
          <span id="stopped" class="glyphicon glyphicon-stop" aria-
hidden="true"></span>
          <span style = "display: none;" id="playing" class="glyphicon
glyphicon-play" aria-hidden="true"></span>
        </span>
      </div>
    </div>
    <script>
      $(".btn").on("click", function(){
        var action = $(this).data("target-action");
        socket.emit('action', action);
      });

      socket.on('status', function (data) {
        if (data === 'playing') {
          $('#stopped').hide();
          $('#playing').show();
        }

        if (data === 'stopped') {
          $('#stopped').show();
          $('#playing').hide();
        }
```

```
        });
      </script>
    </body>
  </html>
```

In the `<head>` tags, you'll find included the source references to jQuery, Bootstrap, and the Socket.IO client libraries; they are all being imported from a **Content Delivery Network (CDN)**, so you don't have to download them.

The `var socket` will hold the Socket.IO client. It will be connecting to the Galileo's server when running `var socket = io('http://ip_address:8080')`. You'll need to replace `ip_address` with your board IP address.

As you can see in the preceding HTML, we are building three buttons. Each of these buttons has a special tag named `data-target-action`. In the later part of the code snippet, we are adding an action listener to all the elements having the class `btn`. By clicking on any of these buttons, the action will be collected from the special data tag and will be emitted to the Socket.IO server under a namespace.

At the bottom of the page, we are adding a current status display, showing a glyph icon, depending on whether an animation is running or not. To receive the real-time updates, we need to listen for a specific event. On this page, we will be listening for the `status` event. When an animation starts `var data`, it will be equal to `playing` and when it stops it, it will be equal to `stopped`. These definitions are created by us.

The following is a table that explains the emitted and listened events in this page:

Events	Data values	Description
`action`	`play` (emitted)	Emitted when user presses the **Play** button. Will be emitted to start an animation.
	`next` (emitted)	Emitted when user presses the **Skip** button. Will be emitted to jump to the next animation.
	`stop` (emitted)	Emitted when user presses the **Stop** button. Will be emitted to stop an animation.
`status`	`playing` (listened)	This event will be received when an animation starts.
	`stopped` (listened)	This event will be received when an animation stops.

This is the protocol we will be using to emit and receive messages in this page. To have a look at the page design, save your code and exit the editor by typing `":wq"` out of the insertion mode (press *Esc* if on insertion mode).

Run the server by typing `node index.js`. When you see **Listening..** printed in the shell, open a browser in your mobile phone (connected to the same network as the Galileo) and type the address: `http://my_ip_address:8080/controls.html`. Replace `my_ip_address` with your Galileo IP address. You should now see the following web page:

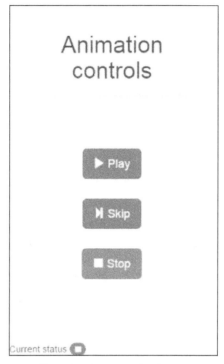

The animation control web page

So far, you'll be able to watch the page that is being served by Galileo, but you won't be able to interact with it yet.

Building the YouTube player page

This page will incorporate a YouTube player with a loaded playlist. We'll be using the `controls.html` web page to emit actions on the animations, and this page will answer to some of these actions. As with the controls page, we'll need to use the Socket.IO client.

 For the YouTube player, we will be using their IFrame API (`https://developers.google.com/youtube/iframe_api_reference`).

Create a new file under the `chapter7` folder using the `vi youtubePlayer.html` command and paste the following code:

```html
<!DOCTYPE html>
<html>
  <head>
    <meta charset="utf-8">
    <meta http-equiv="X-UA-Compatible" content="IE=edge">
    <meta name="viewport" content="width=device-width, initial-scale=1">
    <title>Music Video</title>
    <script src="https://cdnjs.cloudflare.com/ajax/libs/socket.io/1.3.5/socket.io.min.js"></script>
  </head>
  <body>
   <div id="player"></div>
   <script>
      var socket = io('http://192.168.1.79:8080');

      //Setting up player
      var tag = document.createElement('script');
      tag.src = "https://www.youtube.com/iframe_api";
      var firstScriptTag = document.getElementsByTagName('script')[0];
      firstScriptTag.parentNode.insertBefore(tag, firstScriptTag);

      var player;
      function onYouTubeIframeAPIReady() {
        player = new YT.Player('player', {
          height: '390',
          width: '640',
          playerVars: {
            listType: 'playlist',
            list: 'PL-m5kL-HEfO7Q80ewJW4Gl-JeV2aw-1Q_'
          },
          events: {
            'onReady': onPlayerReady,
            'onStateChange': onPlayerStateChange
          }
        });
      }

    function onPlayerReady(event) {
      console.log('Video ready');
    }

    function onPlayerStateChange(change) {
```

```
        // Video started
        if (change.data === 1) socket.emit('video', 'started');

        // Video ended
        if (change.data === -1 || change.data === 0) socket.emit('video',
'stopped');
    }

    socket.on('video', function(msg){

        console.log('message: ' + msg);
        if (msg === 'play') player.playVideo();
        if (msg === 'stop') player.stopVideo();
        if (msg === 'next') player.nextVideo();

    });

    </script>
  </body>
</html>
```

The first thing to do is to replace the address that the Socket.IO client will be connecting to. Replace it with your Galileo IP address.

Moving to the YouTube player, as you can see in their documentation, we need to have a listener for the event that fires when the IFrame API is ready. With it, we can configure many parameters, such as the video width and height or the video/playlist to be loaded:

```
function onYouTubeIframeAPIReady() {
    player = new YT.Player('player', {
        height: '390',
        width: '640',
        playerVars: {
            listType: 'playlist',
            list: 'PL-m5kL-HEfO7Q80ewJW4Gl-JeV2aw-1Q_'
        },
        events: {
            'onReady': onPlayerReady,
            'onStateChange': onPlayerStateChange
        }
    });
}
```

Feel free to change the playlist if you wish. You can do it by replacing the player `var` `list` with the target playlist ID.

It also allows us to declare some event listeners. We will be using the `onStateChange` event to emit the Socket.IO events, while reporting the current status of the video. Inside this event listener, we will receive the value "1" when the video is playing and "-1" or "0" when it is not ready or the video has stopped/ended.

The following are the events we will be emitting and listening to on this page:

Namespace	Data values	Description
`video`	`play` (listened)	When this event is received, the playlist will start playing.
	`next` (listened)	When this event is received, the current video from the playlist will be skipped.
	`stop` (listened)	When this event is received, the player will stop playing.
	started (emitted)	This event will be emitted when a video starts.
	stopped (emitted)	This event will be emitted when a video stops.

Starting your server and opening the URL `http://my_galileo_ip_address:8080/` `player.html` in your computer browser will display to you an embedded YouTube player with a loaded playlist:

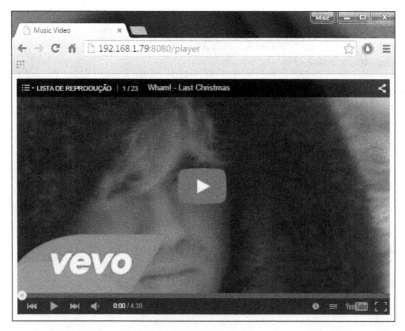

The YouTube player webpage

Launching random LED animations

The one thing that we'll want to do while the videos are playing is to play a random LED animation. To do so, we'll create a new file and develop some methods to help us handle those animations.

The idea is to have a method to stop and set the strip off and the other to select a couple of colors and play an animation, switching between those colors randomly.

To control the LED strip, we will use the lib UPM jsupm_lpd8806 and to loop between the strip LEDs, we will need to use the async module, which will provide us with asynchronous loops. Together with the setTimeout method, this will help us keep the process non-blocking.

Firstly, let's start by installing the async module by typing npm install async inside the project folder (chapter7). When it finishes installing, create a new file by typing vi animations.js and paste the following code:

```
var LPD8806 = require('jsupm_lpd8806').LPD8806;
var async = require('async');

var stripLength = 30;
var ledstrip = new LPD8806(stripLength, 0);

var run = false;

// Obtain a random number between a min and max
function getRandomInt(low, high){
  return Math.floor(Math.random() * (high - low) + low);
}

//Obtain 5 different colors
function getRandomColours() {
  var colours = [];
  for(var i = 0; i != 5; ++i) {
    var r = getRandomInt(0, 255);
    var g = getRandomInt(0, 255);
    var b = getRandomInt(0, 255);
    colours.push({
      red: r,
      green: g,
      blue: b
    })
  }
  return colours;
```

```
}

// Runs animation by switching between the selected set of colours
function runAnimation() {
  run = true;
  var animationColourSet = getRandomColours();
  console.log('animation colours', animationColourSet);
  async.whilst(
    function () {
      // Repeat while run === true
      return run === true;
    },
    function (callback) {
      var colour = animationColourSet[getRandomInt(0,4)];
      fillStripWithColour(colour, callback);
    },
    function (err) {
      console.log('Animation stopped');
    }
  );
}

// Stop animation and set leds off
function stopAnimation() {
  run = false;
  fillStripWithColour({red: 0, green: 0, blue: 0});
}

// Fill strip with a color
var fillStripWithColour = function (colour, callback) {
  for(var i = 0; i != stripLength; ++i) {
    ledstrip.setPixelColor(i, colour.red, colour.green, colour.blue);
  }
  ledstrip.show();
  setTimeout(callback, 300);
}

exports = module.exports = {};
exports.start = runAnimation;
exports.stop = stopAnimation;
```

This code will make two methods available publicly:

- `start`: This selects five random colors and plays an animation by switching between set colors
- `stop`: This stops the current animation that is running and sets the strip off

> In this example, we will only be using a simple light effect. If you wish to create and use more complex effects, take a look at the example available at `https://github.com/muzzley/muzzley-intel-iot-led-strip`. There, you'll find more ideas for light animations and how to accomplish them.

Handling the events in the server

Now that we have animations and our web pages ready, let's handle the emitted events in our server:

- When the user presses the **Play** button in the controls web page, it will emit an event, requesting the animation to start. When the server receives this event, it needs to notify the player to start. By its turn, the player, on changing the status to playing, will emit its current status, which must be captured by the server and used to play the LED strip animation.
- When the user presses the **Stop** button in the controls web page, the server will receive it and will notify the player to stop playing the video. When the player status changes, the server will be notified to stop the LED strip animation.
- When the **Skip** button is pressed in the controls web page, the server stops the LED animation immediately and notifies the player to skip to the next playlist video. On changing the player status, the server will be notified to start the LED animation again.

Edit your `index.js` file by typing `vi index.js` and paste the following code to the end of the file:

```
io.on('connection', function (socket) {
  socket.on('action', function (data) {
    if (data === 'play') io.sockets.emit('video', 'play');
    if (data === 'stop') io.sockets.emit('video', 'stop');
    if(data === 'next') {
      animation.stop();
      // Broadcast to all connected sockets
      io.sockets.emit('video', 'next');
    }
```

```
    });

    socket.on('video', function (data) {
      if (data === 'started') {
        animation.start();
        // Broadcast to all connected sockets
        io.sockets.emit('status', 'playing');
      }

      if (data === 'stopped') {
        animation.stop();
        // Broadcast to all connected sockets
        io.sockets.emit('status', 'stopped');
      }

    });
  });
```

Now we should be able to handle all the events and coordinate all the system. On receiving an event, we'll reply using `io.sockets.emit()`, which allows us to emit an event to all the connected sockets.

On the top of the file, we also need to import the animations file to be able to use it by requiring it and assigning it to a `var`:

```
    var animation = require('./animations');
```

Now we are ready to test the whole system. Start the server with the command `node index.js`. On the same network as Galileo, open a browser in your computer with the URL `http://my_ip_address:8080/player` and another one in your mobile phone with the URL `http://my_ip_address:8080/controls`.

Using the control web page in your mobile phone, you'll be able to start, stop, or skip the animations along with the music videos.

Summary

In this chapter, we learned how to obtain bidirectional real-time interaction using Galileo. We started to wire and control an LPD8806 LED strip from our board and progressively created a server to handle the requests and the real-time events. Together using the YouTube IFrame Player, we were able to coordinate animations from the Galileo while being controlled from a web page.

In the next chapter, we'll explore the Intel® XDK IoT Edition development environment, and see how we can use it to create applications for Intel® Galileo.

8
The Intel XDK IoT Edition

So far, you have seen the three different tools to develop your connected applications: the Arduino IDE, Wyliodrin, and vi. In this chapter, we will approach a more complete solution, the **Intel XDK IoT Edition**. It is an end-to-end IoT development solution. It allows you to not only develop Node.js IoT applications, but also to easily deploy them in your board and install all the required external packages. It also allows you to create companion mobile apps by making design, test, and deployment tools available. In this chapter, we'll have a look at the main features this IDE provides and how we can use it to run an example app.

In this chapter, you'll learn about:

- Installing Intel XDK IoT Edition and connecting your development board
- Understanding the platform perks and tools
- Developing and running an IoT app on the Galileo board
- Developing a companion app and using it from your mobile devices

Introducing Intel XDK

The Intel XDK is an interesting development platform. It allows you to create, debug, and run tools for JavaScript applications. It is a complete development solution and a great help when developing your Intel Galileo projects.

This platform helps you develop your IoT projects faster. It can also help you in debugging and running your projects straight on to Galileo. It already contains many useful examples using the Grove Starter Kit sensors. It also has a strong mobile component through the companion apps. To use it, you'll just need to have a basic knowledge of JavaScript and HTML5.

Let's install and take a look at it. Visit `https://software.intel.com/en-us/html5/xdk-iot`, select your operating system in the green box, and download it. let's take a look at the various ways to be taken into account when installing this software on different OSes:

- **Windows**: Right click on the downloaded file and select **Run as administrator**. After the installation is complete, you'll need to install the Bonjour Print Services. It enables Intel XDK IoT Edition to automatically detect the boards connected to your network. To do so, visit `https://support.apple.com/kb/DL999?locale=en_US`. Download and install it.

- **Linux**: Open a terminal and navigate to your downloads folder. Extract the files using the `tar zxvf downloaded_file_name` command. Navigate to the extracted folder and type `./install`.

- **Mac OS**: Extract the installer by clicking on the `.dmg` file you just downloaded. Install the XDK by double-clicking on the extracted `.pkg` file.

Run the Intel XDK IoT Edition. You'll need to have a developer account in order to use it. Click on **Need to sign up for an account?** and fill in the form to create one. Log in with your credentials.

Creating and deploying an IoT project on Galileo

In the new project view, on the left-hand side under the **INTERNET OF THINGS EMBEDDED APPLICATION** tab, you'll find two options: **Templates** and **Import Your Node.js Project**. Click on the **Templates** option, and you'll see a list of project templates.

We'll be using the **Touch Notifier** template. Click on it and then on the **Continue** button. The next thing to do is name your project. Feel free to name it as you wish, but we'll be naming it `iot-doorbell`.

As soon as the project has downloaded and opened, you'll have the following workspace:

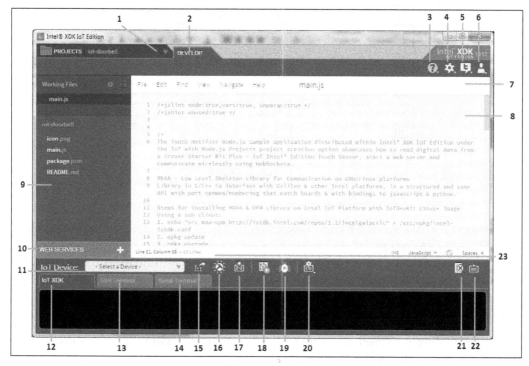

The IoT app editor

Here you can find the following key options:

Serial number	Features
1	Project selector
2	Development mode
3	Help
4	Settings
5	Twitter feed
6	Account options
7	File options
8	Code editor
9	Project files
10	Web services integration
11	Board selection
12	App log

Serial number	Features
13	**SSH Terminal**
14	**Serial Terminal**
15	Upload app
16	Build app
17	Stop app
18	Run app
19	Debug app
20	Deployment manager
21	Clear console
22	Toggle console
23	File stats and errors

This demo app consists of a touch sensor that will trigger a buzzer. In the project files (point 9 in the preceding list), click on `main.js`. Looking at the code (point 8), you'll see that this app runs a server with Socket.IO to enable real-time message exchanges. Whenever the touch sensor is pressed, the buzzer will make some noise and the connected Socket.IO clients will also be notified. For this demo, we'll be using two sensors from the Grove Starter Kit: the buzzer and the touch sensor.

With your Galileo powered off, connect the Grove base shield to it, connecting the buzzer to D6 and the touch sensor to D2:

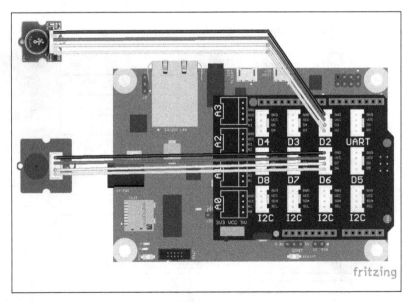

The IoT demo app wiring

Insert your IoT Dev Kit image into the SD card slot and power on your Galileo.

Now it's time to connect our board to the XDK. In the IoT device selector (point 11), you should see your board listed after powering up. If your Galileo is not displayed in the list, select the **[+] Add Manual Connection** option. For this, you'll need to know your device's IP address. You can run a Wyliodrin shell and execute the `ifconfig` command in order to find it. Once you know your IP address, insert it in the pop-up window in the **Address:** field and click on the **Connect** button. If everything went right, you'll see a pop-up window saying **Connected**.

All the project library dependencies and versions can be found in the `package.json` file. If you click on the file, you'll find the Socket.IO dependency added to our project.

Install the project dependencies by clicking on the build button (point 16). This process takes some time to conclude, and you can follow what's happening by looking at the app logs (point 12). You'll just need to build it once, unless you add new external dependencies to the project. Whenever you make changes in your files, you'll just need to save (inside point 7 in the preceding list, click on **File | Save**), upload (point 15), and run the project (point 18).

When the installation is complete, run the project by clicking on the Run button (point 18). At this point, your project is running on your Galileo board. The touch sensor won't be read without the existence of a Socket.IO client connection, and to do so, we'll create a companion app.

Creating a companion app

Click on the project selector (point 1) and choose **+ New Project**. Under the **HTML5 COMPANION HYBRID MOBILE OR WEB APP** tab, click on **Samples and Demos** and then on **General**. On the right-hand side of the window, you'll find two options: **Standard HTML5** and **HTML5 + Cordova**. Click on the second one and choose the **Touch Notifier** companion app project. Name your companion app project. We'll be naming it `doorbell-mobile`.

Now you'll see that your workspace has changed a bit:

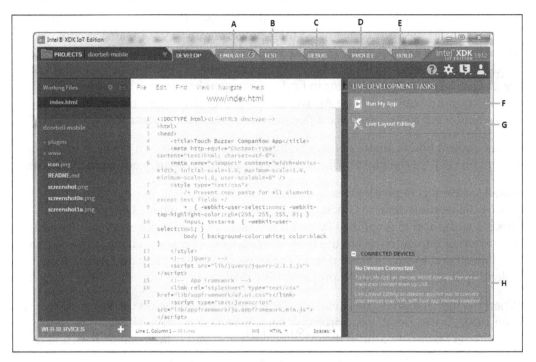

The companion app development workspace

Here you can find the following key components:

Options	Features
A	Emulate app
B	Test app
C	Debug app
D	Profiling
E	Build mobile app
F	Run mobile app
G	App interface editor
H	Connected mobile devices

As you can see, there are many options available. Let's start by testing the emulation (point A in the preceding list) option by clicking on it. Here, you are able to select a mobile device and the display orientation, using it as a real device when interacting with your IoT app.

By now you should see the first HTML page displayed on your screen:

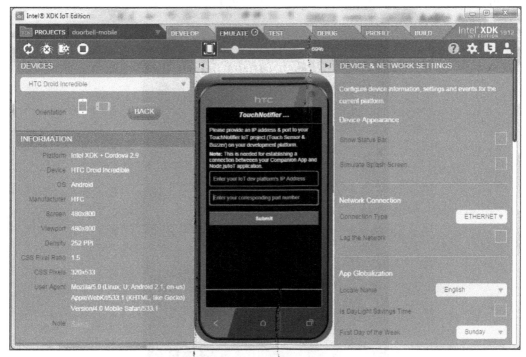

Emulating the companion app

Enter your board's IP address and in the port number, insert 1337, which is the port your IoT app server is listening to. Now you can finally press the touch sensor connected to Galileo. Touch it and you'll hear the buzzer ringing and see the emulated app displaying a message to check your door.

Now let's test it using a real mobile device. Grab your smartphone or tablet and install the Intel App previewer from one of the popular app stores.

In the XDK, click on the **TEST** tab (point B), and you'll be asked if you want to push your files to the testing server. If you do so, you'll have your app available right away inside the Intel App previewer. Another option is to just scan the displayed QR code.

Open the Intel App previewer on your mobile device and log in with your developer account credentials. If you pushed the app files to the test server, you'll find your app listed under the **Server Apps** tab. If you didn't push your files, click on the camera button on the top-right of the app and scan the displayed QR code.

The companion app should now be running on your device. Insert the IP address and the app server port (1337), and you'll find your app waiting for the buzzer to ring:

Running the companion app as a mobile app

Try pressing the touch sensor and take a look at your mobile device. It should be displaying the message you saw earlier.

Summary

The Intel XDK IoT Edition is a powerful and complete tool that allows Galileo developers to easily create IoT applications. Besides making the development fast, it easily connects with the mobile world.

In this chapter, we had a small walkthrough of its main features by creating a doorbell ring notifier, which notifies the user's mobile device when the ring is played.

In the next chapter, we'll be using this development tool to create a more complex example—developing an IoT quiz game and using mobile companion apps to play it.

9
Developing an IoT Quiz

Now that you are a bit more familiar with the Intel XDK IoT Edition, let's use it to build a more complex project. In this chapter, we will be using everything we've learned so far to develop a project from scratch. Combining the perks of real-time communication with actuators, we'll create an IoT multiplayer quiz, a simple game served by Intel Galileo and played on mobile devices.

In this chapter, you'll learn about:

- Using an LCD and a buzzer to improve the game experience
- Using a key value storage system to cache data
- Coordinating multiple remote devices using a Galileo board
- Building a mobile app

Required component

For this project, besides the Intel Galileo board, power supply unit, and the Grove base shield, you'll need the following components:

- **Grove LCD RGB Backlight**: It is a part of the Grove Starter Kit Plus, and is a 16 x 2 LCD screen. It brings more functionalities than most typical LCD screens. Besides allowing us to print two rows of 16 characters at most, the backlight can also be RGB customizable.

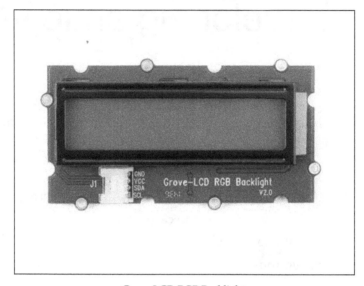

Grove LCD RGB Backlight

It also supports user-defined characters and communicates using the I2C protocol (`https://learn.sparkfun.com/tutorials/i2c`) through only two IOs.

 You can find more details about this component at
`http://www.seeedstudio.com/depot/Grove-LCD-RGB-Backlight-p-1643.html`.

- **Grove Buzzer**: This is the same buzzer we used in the previous chapter. It is also a part of the Grove Starter Kit Plus.

Grove Buzzer

It can be connected to a digital output to simply emit sound, or it can be connected to a PWM output and play different tones.

 You can find more details about this component at http://www.seeedstudio.com/depot/Grove-Buzzer-p-768.html.

Creating the Galileo app

In this project, we will be using the aforementioned components to improve the game experience. We'll use the LCD screen to display game information such as the Galileo IP address, which will be used to pair the mobile devices with the game or the current questions round. The buzzer will be used to notify the users that the game or a new question round has just started.

You should connect them to your board by referring to the following image:

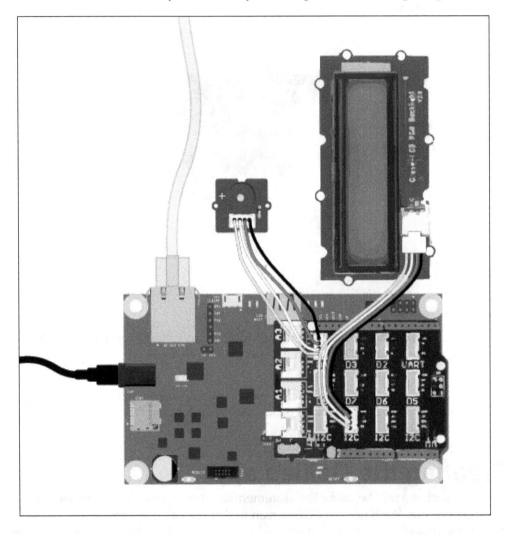

First, attach the base shield to your board. Connect the LCD screen to the I2C connector, just like in the preceding image, and the buzzer to the digital connector D4.

Connect your Galileo to the Internet using an Ethernet cable connection or you may use a wireless connection.

With the basic setup finished, download the game source files from the Packt Publishing website (http://www.packtpub.com/support). Open the Intel XDK and then open the **IoT-quiz** project by navigating to **PROJECTS | Open an Intel XDK project** and selecting the file IoT-quiz.xdk inside the project folder.

This app will run in Galileo and handle the players' connections, cache their results, and coordinate the LCD and buzzer according to the game stage. Let's take a deeper look at the concepts behind this game.

Coordinating players

The player's coordination will be done using the Socket.IO real-time engine. The first thing we should do is define the messages we will be exchanging between the server (Galileo) and clients (mobile devices). Here, we'll create four main stages after a client connects. In the following image, we can find four different colored stages. The first stage (green) is registering new players in the game, the second stage (blue) is the questions being presented and answered, the third stage (orange) is displaying the correct answer, and the fourth stage (red) is displaying the high scores.

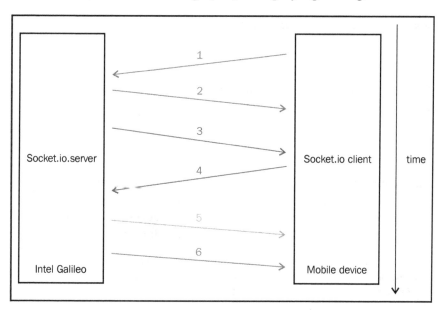

From the preceding diagram, you can observe the flow in the following manner:

1. Player requests to join the game.
2. Server replies with a success true/false.
3. Server sends the question and answer options to the mobile devices (clients).
4. Client selects the answer and informs the server.
5. Server sends the right answer to the clients.
6. Server sends the game results to the clients.

Keeping this in mind, in the `main.js` file, you'll find the Socket.IO server being set up and listening for new connections:

```
var app = http.createServer(function (req, res) {
  'use strict';
  res.writeHead(200, {'Content-Type': 'text/plain'});
  res.end('<h1>Hello world from Intel IoT platform!</h1>');
}).listen(1337);

var io = require('socket.io')(app);

//Attach a 'connection' event handler to the server
io.on('connection', function (socket) {
    ...

  socket.on('error', function (error) {
    ...
  });

  //Attach a 'disconnect' event handler to the socket
  socket.on('disconnect', function () {
    ...
  });
});
```

Every time a connection is successfully established, Galileo will be waiting for a client to send the registration message to join the game. If the game hasn't started yet, the new player will be added to a player list, and the server will confirm the client through a callback that he/she was successfully registered:

```
socket.on('register_player', function (player, callback) {
    if (game.isGameRunning()) return callback(null, {success:
      false, message: 'Game already started. Try again later'});

    // Add the player to the game
    game.registerPlayer(player.name, socket);

    // Replying to mobile device, game registration request
    callback(null, {success: true});

    // If is the first player to join, launch a timer to start the
      game
    if (game.players.length === 1) {
```

```
        console.log('Game will start in Xs');
        startGameTimer = setTimeout(game.start, 3000);
    }
  });
```

The returned message will be using the following parameters:

- **Error**: If an error is present, it should be sent using the callback's first parameter

- **Message**: The message structure should be {success: true/false, message: 'optional'}

To help us keep track of players' data and easily exchange data messages, we are using a custom object that we have named `Player`. This object has a name, a connection socket, and a unique ID, referring to the socket ID. It can emit events to a specific client, such as the questions, correct answer, and game scores:

```
function Player (options) {
   this.name = options.name;
   this.socket = options.socket;
   this.id = options.socket.id;
}

// Send scores to player
Player.prototype.displayScores = function (scores) {
   this.socket.emit('scores', {gameScore: scores});
},

// Display the question answer
Player.prototype.showCorrectAnswer = function (correctAnswer) {
   this.socket.emit('display_right_answer', {correctAnswer:
     correctAnswer});
};

// Send question to player and return the answer
Player.prototype.sendQuestion = function (question, timeout,
   roundNumber, callback) {
   this.socket.emit('question', {question: question, timeout:
     timeout, round: roundNumber}, callback);
};

module.exports = Player;
```

The game engine

The game engine can be found in the game.js file located inside the lib folder. Game and players' data will be handled here:

```
var players = [];
var questions, roundNumber = null;
var gameRunning = false;
```

All the players joining and leaving the game will be added or removed from the players' array. The var gameRunning value will indicate whether the game is already running or not. The vars questions and roundNumber values will store the game questions and the current question round number, respectively.

Game questions will be stored in a static JSON file, containing an array of questions. This file is named questions.json. You can add or change questions as long as the question structure is kept:

```
[
    {
        "id": 1,
        "question": "Which one is an Internet of Things
            major concern?",
        "answers": {
            "A": "Security",
            "B": "Too many devices connected to the Internet",
            "C": "Sedentarism",
            "D": "Not enought storage available in the world"
        },
        "correctAnswer": "A"
    },
    {
        "id": 2,
        "question": "What can you sense when using this
            Grove sensor?",
        "url": "http://www.seeedstudio.com/depot/bmz_cache/
            9/9b57087d562b65bcd9d77059b16061eb.image.530x397.jpg",
        "answers": {
            "A": "Light",
            "B": "Temperature",
            "C": "Moisture",
            "D": "Sound"
        },
        "correctAnswer": "D"
    }
]
```

The first one is a text only question and the second one a question with an image.

Whenever there's a single player connected, a countdown timer will start. Other players who want to join the current game will need to do it during this countdown. When the time limit is reached, the game starts by calling the following method, which can be found in the game.js file:

```
exports.start = function () {
  gameRunning = true;
  roundNumber = 1;

    // Load questions from a JSON file
    fs.readFile(''/home/root/.node_app_slot/questions.json'',
      ''utf8'', function (err, data) {
      if (err) throw err;
      questions = JSON.parse(data);


      async.whilst(
        function () {
          // While round number is not the last one and there are
            connected players, keep playing
          return (roundNumber <= questions.length &&
            players.length > 0);
        },

        // Start next question round
        nextQuestionRound,

        // When all rounds end
        function () {

            for (var i = 0; i != players.length; ++i) {
              players[i].displayScores(scores);
            }
            gameRunning = false;
        }
      );
    });
};
```

In `game.js`, we can also find the preceding method, which is responsible to start the game. The game status control variable will be checked as true and the round number will be set to the first one. The game starts by loading all the questions from the JSON file. Galileo will then asynchronously keep on processing the question rounds until it cycles all the questions or all the players leave the game.

 To accomplish this, we used the `async` library (`https://github.com/caolan/async`).

The `async.whilst` method will lock every `nextQuestionRound(callback)` function until its callback is called:

```
function nextQuestionRound(callback) {
  // Send the round question to all players
  async.each(players, function (player, playerDone) {

    // Set a maximum time to wait for the question answer
    var questionTimer = setTimeout(function () {
      console.log(''ANSWER was not answered'');
      return playerDone();
    }, 15000);

    // Question and options to send to the mobile device
    var roundQuestion = {
      question: questions[roundNumber-1].question,
      answers: questions[roundNumber-1].answers,
      url: questions[roundNumber-1].url
    }

    player.sendQuestion(roundQuestion, 15000, roundNumber,
      function (err, answer) {

      // Cancel the timer since the question was answered
      clearTimeout(questionTimer);

      // Evaluate question
      if (answer !== questions[roundNumber-1].correctAnswer) {
        // If answer is wrong, return and release
        return playerDone();
      }
      // If answer is correct, increase score and return and
        release
      scores.increaseScore(player.name, playerDone);
    });
```

```
    },

    // When all players are done in current round
    function () {
      for (var i = 0; i != players.length; ++i) {
        players[i].showCorrectAnswer(questions[roundNumber-
          1].correctAnswer);
    }

    setTimeout(function () {
        ++roundNumber;
        callback();
      }, 3000);
    });
  }
```

This method is our game core. Here, we'll be using the `async.each` method to asynchronously loop the game participants in parallel. Each participant will be sent the game round question. Each player's answer is expected to be returned in 15 seconds or it will be considered unanswered. The `playerDone` callback will be called every time a player finishes "his move" in the current round. It will be called when a player answers the question correctly or incorrectly, or it will be called if the player doesn't answer the question at all.

When all the `playerDone` callbacks are called for all the players, the correct answer will be displayed to all the players for 3 seconds. Then the round number will increase by one unit and, on returning the round callback, a new round will be processed in the previous `async.whilst` loop.

Caching the results

Every time a player answers a displayed question correctly, his score will increase by one unit. We'll keep this data structurally cached using **Redis**. The Intel IoT Dev Kit image already comes with it installed, so you'll be ready to use it. Redis is a key-value cache and storage system, where you can store your data by type (http://redis.io/).

Inside `lib/storage.js`, you can find the methods for our small storage system that use the Redis Node.js client (https://github.com/mranney/node_redis). We'll use sorted sets to store our data (http://redis.io/commands#sorted_set). Having a set key, we can add multiple members with an associated score. Here, we will use the players' IDs as members and their current scores as member scores:

```
var redis = require('redis');
var storage = redis.createClient();

// Key where we'll be storing our game score data
var storageKey = 'iot-quiz:scores';

exports = module.exports = {};

exports.increaseScore = function (playerKey, callback) {
  storage.zincrby(storageKey, 1, playerKey, callback);
};

// Get total correct answers
exports.getScores = function (callback) {
  storage.zrevrange(storageKey, 0, -1, 'WITHSCORES', function
    (err, score) {
    return callback(err, score);
  });
}

exports.clear = function (callback) {
  storage.del(storageKey, callback);
};
```

The `clear` method will be used every time a new game starts to clear the last game's scores, if they exist. Whenever a player answers a question correctly, we'll increase its score using the `zincrby` method (http://redis.io/commands/ZINCRBY).

To retrieve stored data, we can list it by score. Using the `zrevrange` method (http://redis.io/commands/zrevrange) will return us an array of members in descending order, starting with the player IDs that have the best scores. The `WITHSCORES` option will also include the player scores in the results, returning the score value in the array. This will be used to display the game scores at the end of the game.

Using the LCD and buzzer

Pretty much like in the previous chapter's example, we will use a buzzer to help improve the game experience. Using the MRAA library, we'll export and use GPIO 4, where the buzzer should be connected:

```
var mraa = require("mraa");
var buzzer_pin = new mraa.Gpio(4);
buzzer_pin.dir(mraa.DIR_OUT);
buzzer_pin.write(0);

exports = module.exports = {};

exports.playBuzzer = function (time) {
  buzzer_pin.write(1);
  setTimeout(function () {
    buzzer_pin.write(0);
  }, time);
}
```

When a game starts or whenever a new question is displayed, the buzzer will make some noise for some short time interval. Although we are just using the buzzer to alert the players, if you prefer, you can use fancy sounds and create melodies using the buzzer **UPM** module (http://iotdk.intel.com/docs/master/upm/node/classes/buzzer.html).

The Grove LCD will be controlled using the UPM library. It will be useful to display the Galileo IP address and the rounds status:

```
var LCD  = require(''jsupm_i2clcd'');
var os = require( ''os'' );
var myLCD = new LCD.Jhd1313m1(0, 0x3E, 0x62);

exports = module.exports = {};


exports.printRound = function (roundNumber, total) {
  myLCD.clear();
  myLCD.setCursor(0,0);
  myLCD.write("Current round:");
  myLCD.setCursor(1,0);
  var roundInfo = roundNumber + "/" + total;
  myLCD.write(roundInfo);
};
```

External dependencies

Some Node.js libraries dependencies are already installed in the Developer Kit image, but the ones that aren't have to be included in the `package.json` file:

```
{
  "name": "IoT-Quiz",
  "description": "A quiz served by Galileo and played with mobile
devices",
  "author": "Miguel Sousa <r.miguel.f.sousa@gmail.com>",
  "version": "0.0.1",
  "main": "main.js",
  "engines": {
    "node": """>=0.10.0""
  },
  "dependencies": {
    "async": "0.9.x",
  "redis": "0.12.x"
  }
}
```

The preceding JSON file contains our project description and libraries dependencies with version. When you press the XDK build project button, this file will be read and the dependencies written on it will be installed.

Creating the companion app

Now, let's take a look at the mobile project. From the PACKT publishing downloaded code, open the project `IoT-Quiz_client.xdk`, located inside the folder with the same name.

This project contains the mobile companion app, built using HTML5 and Cordova, and also with the help of the Intel App Framework (http://app-framework-software.intel.com/api.php).

Interface

Using the drag and drop visual editor, we created the following page structure:

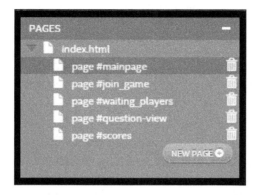

Each of the following "pages" were built for specific game events:

- **#mainpage**: This is the landing page. This view displays the form to insert the Galileo Socket.IO server IP address.

- **#join_game**: In this view, we'll enter our name. After submitting it, we'll join the game or be alerted that the game has already started.

- **#waiting_players**: It is displayed while a player is waiting for the game to start.

- **#question_view**: Here, questions and answer options will be displayed.

- **#scores**: This last page lists the players' game scores.

All the HTML content is located in the `index.html` file. The editor-generated stylesheets can be found inside the `css/index/styles` folder.

User handlers

User handlers, by default, are located in `scripts/index_user_scripts.js`. Here, we'll define the click behavior for each of the following buttons:

- **Connect button**: This button will make the mobile device connect to the Galileo server. If the device connects successfully, the next UI page will be loaded. In order to move to the **Insert name** page, we are using Intel's App Framework, `$.ui.loadContent`. If the connection fails, an alert box will be displayed:

```
$(document).on("click", "#connect_button", function (evt) {

    $('#connecting-loader').show();
```

```
var ipAddress = $('#ip_address').val();

connect(ipAddress, function (err) {
  $('#connecting-loader').hide();
if (err) {
    alert('Failed to connect');
    } else {
      $.ui.loadContent("#join_game", false, false,
        "slide");
}
  });
});
```

- **Submit name button**: In the second view, we'll find the submit name button. Clicking on this button will result in sending the player name to the Galileo server and obtaining a confirmation whether or not the player is participating in the game. If there's a game already going on, the player will be notified and disconnected. If the player joins the game successfully, he will be moved to the **waiting players** view:

```
$(document).on("click", "#submit_name_button", function (evt)
{
    var playerName = $('#player_name').val();
    socket.emit('register_player', {name: playerName}, function
(err, response) {
        if (err || !response || !response.success) {
          alert('Game already started. Try again later..');
          disconnect();
          return;
      }
    $.ui.loadContent("#waiting_players", false, false, "slide");
    });
});
```

- **Answer question button**: When a question is displayed, this will be the event attached to each possible answer. The submitted answer will be retrieved by collecting the data-answerkey element contained in every answer option and matching the answer code:

```
$('.question-answer').click(function(evt) {
    $(this).css('background-color', 'red');
    var answer = $(this).data("answerkey");
    answerQuestion(answer);
});
```

Game handlers

The game handlers can be found inside the app.js file, located at www/js. These handlers process receive socket events from Galileo.

After a socket connection is successfully established, the client will listen for three main events:

- **Display question**: This event will make the mobile client clear and display the round question and possible answers. It will start a figurative countdown timer and assign the callback to another variable so that it can be called when the player answers the question:

```
socket.on("question", function (message, callback) {
    clearQuestion();
    $.ui.unblockUI();
    $.ui.loadContent("#question-view", false, false,
      "slide");
    currentQuestion = message.question;
    selectedAnswer = null;
    startTimer(message.timeout);
    setQuestionDisplay(message.question, message.round);
    answerReply = callback;
});
```

- **Display right answer**: When this event is received, the client will highlight the correct answer in green:

```
socket.on("display_right_answer", function (message) {
    stopTimer();
    $('#answer-'+ message.correctAnswer).css('background-
      color', '#98FB98');
    if (message.correctAnswer !== selectedAnswer) {
      $('#answer-'+selectedAnswer).css('background-
        color', '#ec8287');
    }
});
```

- **Display game scores**: When this event is received, the scores list will be displayed. The score variables is a Redis array result. It contains mixed value types, player IDs, and player scores:

```
socket.on('scores', function (scores) {
    $.ui.loadContent("#scores", false, false, "slide");
    for (var i = 0; i != scores.gameScore.length; ++i) {
      if (i%2 === 0) {
        var place = i + 1;
```

```
        $('#scores-list').append(''<li class="widget
          uib_w_22" data-uib="app_framework/listitem"
          data-ver="1">'+place+'. '+scores.gameScore[i]+'
          ('+scores.gameScore[i+1]+')'+'</li>');
    }
  }
  setTimeout(function () {
  socket.disconnect();
  $.ui.unblockUI();
      }, 5000);
    });
  }catch(e) {
    alert(e);
  }
}
```

Building the mobile app

To build the mobile app, at the top of the XDK, click on the **Build** tab. Here, you'll find multiple platforms available. Feel free to build the Windows 8 Phone app (https://software.intel.com/en-us/xdk/docs/tut-build-win8phone) or iOS (https://software.intel.com/en-us/xdk/docs/tut-build-binary-ios), but here, we will only be doing it for Android.

If you have access to an Android device, select the Android legacy hybrid app build.

You'll be shown a build page containing many options for your build, such as required plugins or even icons images. For this demo, no plugins are necessary to install. Configure the app build as you wish and when you are ready, click on **Build App Now**. As soon as the app is built, check your e-mail; your app will be there. If you wish to, you can send it to multiple e-mail accounts. Allow your mobile device to install apps from unknown sources, open your e-mail in the device, and download the file that was sent to you. Click on it to install it.

Running the game

Open the IoT Quiz project and make sure the project is running on Galileo and with all the dependencies installed. Select your device from the devices list or add it manually if it's not listed. Upload the code to Galileo and press the **Install/Build** button. Run the app by clicking on the **Run** button. The Galileo IP address should now be displayed on the LCD screen.

Open the **Emulate** tab in your XDK and the mobile app you just downloaded in order to have two clients. Insert the IP address in both devices:

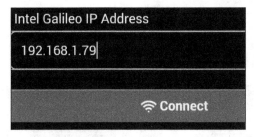

Inserting the IP address

Next, insert the name:

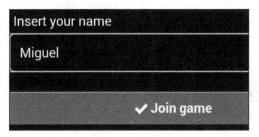

Inserting players name

As soon as the game countdown timer finishes, the buzzer will sound and both devices will receive the first question. When all the devices finish answering the question, the correct answer will be displayed:

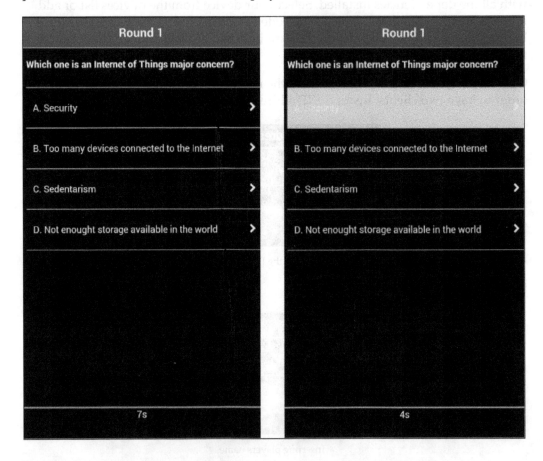

Try to answer all the questions until the final round. When all the questions are answered, the scores will be displayed. Then the game will end and all the players will be disconnected. If you want to play again, you'll have to repeat the registration process.

Summary

In this chapter, we built a more complex project with the help of Intel tools.

We've created an IoT Quiz multiplayer game, played on mobile devices and served by a Galileo board. Galileo provided the game information to an LCD and used a buzzer to alert players for new questions being displayed. Also, with the help of a storage system, we were able to keep our data stored and organized, ready to be displayed on request.

In the next chapter, we'll go a bit further and integrate a device with an IoT cloud.

10
Integrating with Muzzley

One identified issue regarding IoT is that there will be lots of connected devices and each one speaks its own language, not sharing the same protocols with other devices. This leads to an increasing number of apps to control each of those devices. Every time you purchase connected products, you'll be required to have the exclusive product app, and, in the near future, where it is predicted that more devices will be connected to the Internet than people, this is indeed a problem, which is known as the basket of remotes.

Many solutions have been appearing for this problem. Some of them focus on creating common communication standards between the devices or even creating their own protocol such as the Intel **Common Connectivity Framework** (**CCF**). A different approach consists in predicting the device's interactions, where collected data is used to predict and trigger actions on the specific devices. An example using this approach is Muzzley. It not only supports a common way to speak with the devices, but also learns from the users' interaction, allowing them to control all their devices from a common app, and on collecting usage data, it can predict users' actions and even make different devices work together.

In this chapter, we will start by understanding what Muzzley is and how we can integrate with it. We will then do some development to allow you to control your own building's entrance door. For this purpose, we will use Galileo as a bridge to communicate with a relay and the Muzzley cloud, allowing you to control the door from a common mobile app and from anywhere as long as there is Internet access. Finally, you'll learn how to use the Muzzley app to define rules and make the homemade system communicate with the existing connected devices available in stores.

In this chapter, you'll learn about:

- Setting up a Muzzley app and profile
- Integrating with Muzzley
- Building your own control interface
- Controlling your building's entrance door with Muzzley
- Using Muzzley workers to make different devices work together

Wiring the circuit

In this chapter, we'll be using a real home AC inter-communicator with a building entrance door unlock button and this will require you to do some homework. This integration will require you to open your inter-communicator and adjust the inner circuit, so be aware that there are always risks of damaging it.

If you don't want to use a real inter-communicator, you can replace it by an LED or even by the buzzer module we used in the previous chapter. If you want to use a real device, you can use a DC inter-communicator, but in this guide, we'll only be explaining how to do the wiring using an AC inter-communicator.

The first thing you have to do is to take a look at the device manual and check whether it works with AC current, and the voltage it requires. If you can't locate your product manual, search for it online.

In this chapter, we'll be using the solid state relay we previously used in *Chapter 4, Creating a Motion Sensing Light*. This relay accepts a voltage range from 24 V up to 380 V AC, and your inter-communicator should also work in this voltage range.

Like we used in the earlier chapters, you'll also need some electrical wires and electrical wires junctions.

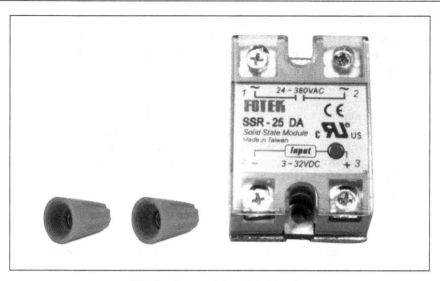

Wire junctions and the solid state relay

This equipment will be used to adapt the door unlocking circuit to allow it to be controlled from the Galileo board using a relay.

The main idea is to use a relay to close the door opener circuit, resulting in the door being unlocked. This can be accomplished by joining the inter-communicator switch wires with the relay wires. Use some wire and wire junctions to do it, as displayed in the following image:

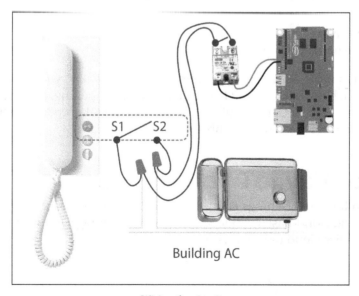

Wiring the circuit

The building/house AC circuit is represented in yellow, and **S1** and **S2** represent the inter-communicator switch (button). On pressing the button, we will also be closing this circuit, and the door will be unlocked. This way, the lock can be controlled both ways, using the original button and the relay.

Before starting to wire the circuit, make sure that the inter-communicator circuit is powered off. If you can't switch it off, you can always turn off your house electrical board for a couple of minutes. Make sure that it is powered off by pressing the unlock button and trying to open the door.

If you are not sure of what you must do or don't feel comfortable doing it, ask for help from someone more experienced.

Open your inter-communicator, locate the switch, and perform the changes displayed in the preceding image (you may have to do some soldering).

The Intel Galileo board will then activate the relay using pin 13, where you should wire it to the relay's connector number 3, and the Galileo's ground (GND) should be connected to the relay's connector number 4.

Beware that not all the inter-communicator circuits work the same way and although we try to provide a general way to do it, there're always the risk of damaging your device or being electrocuted. Do it at your own risk.

Power on your inter-communicator circuit and check whether you can open the door by pressing the unlock door button.

If you prefer not using the inter-communicator with the relay, you can always replace it with a buzzer or an LED to simulate the door opening. Also, since the relay is connected to Galileo's pin 13, with the same relay code, you'll have visual feedback from the Galileo's onboard LED.

The Muzzley IoT ecosystem

Muzzley is an Internet of Things ecosystem that is composed of connected devices, mobile apps, and cloud-based services. Devices can be integrated with Muzzley through the device cloud or the device itself:

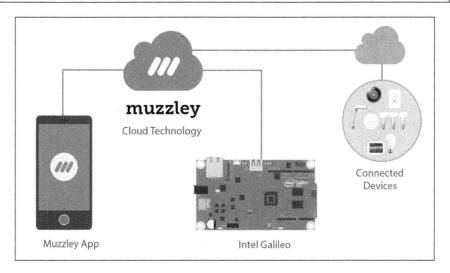

It offers device control, a rules system, and a machine learning system that predicts and suggests actions, based on the device usage.

The mobile app is available for Android, iOS, and Windows phone. It can pack all your Internet-connected devices in to a single common app, allowing them to be controlled together, and to work with other devices that are available in real-world stores or even other homemade connected devices, like the one we will create in this chapter.

Muzzley is known for being one of the first generation platforms with the ability to predict a users' actions by learning from the user's interaction with their own devices.

Human behavior is mostly unpredictable, but for convenience, people end up creating routines in their daily lives. The interaction with home devices is an example where human behavior can be observed and learned by an automated system.

Muzzley tries to take advantage of these behaviors by identifying the user's recurrent routines and making suggestions that could accelerate and simplify the interaction with the mobile app and devices. Devices that don't know of each others' existence get connected through the user behavior and may create synergies among themselves.

When the user starts using the Muzzley app, the interaction is observed by a profiler agent that tries to acquire a behavioral network of the linked cause-effect events. When the frequency of these network associations becomes important enough, the profiler agent emits a suggestion for the user to act upon. For instance, if every time a user arrives home, he switches on the house lights, check the thermostat, and adjust the air conditioner accordingly, the profiler agent will emit a set of suggestions based on this. The cause of the suggestion is identified and shortcuts are offered for the effect-associated action. For instance, the user could receive in the Muzzley app the following suggestions: "You are arriving at a known location. Every time you arrive here, you switch on the «Entrance bulb». Would you like to do it now?"; or "You are arriving at a known location. The thermostat «Living room» says that the temperature is at 15 degrees Celsius. Would you like to set your «Living room» air conditioner to 21 degrees Celsius?"

When it comes to security and privacy, Muzzley takes it seriously and all the collected data is used exclusively to analyze behaviors to help make your life easier.

This is the system where we will be integrating our door unlocker. In this chapter, we will integrate our device with the Muzzley cloud using Galileo as a bridge (gateway) to communicate between the lock and this ecosystem. Galileo will answer Muzzley requests and will act on the unlocking system, unlocking the entrance door.

Creating a Muzzley app

The first step is to own a Muzzley developer account.

 If you don't have one yet, you can obtain one by visiting `https://muzzley.com/developers`, clicking on the **Sign up** button, and submitting the displayed form.

To create an app, click on the top menu option **Apps** and then **Create app**. Name your App **Galileo Lock** and if you want to, add a description to your project.

As soon as you click on **Submit**, you'll see two buttons displayed, allowing you to select the integration type:

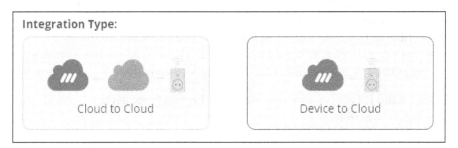

Muzzley allows you to integrate through the product manufacturer cloud or directly with a device. In this example, we will be integrating directly with the device. To do so, click on **Device to Cloud** integration.

Fill in the provider name as you wish and pick two image URLs to be used as the profile (for example, `http://www.bestsquarefeet.com/wp-content/uploads/2013/01/Commercial1.jpg`) and channel (for example, `http://png-2.findicons.com/files/icons/949/token/256/lock.png`) images.

We can select one of two available ways to add our device: it can be done using UPnP discovery or by inserting a custom serial number. Pick the device discovery option **Serial number** and ignore the fields **Interface UUID** and **Email Access List**; we will come back for them later. Save your changes by pressing the **Save changes** button.

Creating the device integration profile

To be able to communicate under a common language, we'll need to define the hierarchical structure of our device components and the respective properties. In this integration, we will only have a door lock, which will be our only type of component. The only information we need to exchange about this type of component will be the door status, and this will be our only property.

On the app details web page, in the top-left corner, you'll find the **Profile Spec** option. Click on it, and let's create our integration profile.

On this page, you'll find a section named **Component #1**. This is where we'll define our first and only component. Click on the arrow to expand the component section and insert the key `door-lock` in the **ID** field. This ID should be a suggestive key name since it will identify the lock component type. Fill in the label with the name of the component, and pick any name that will help you remember the type of component that you are creating.

Now let's define the properties. Expand the **Property #1** section and set `lock-status` as the property **ID**, also giving this property a **Label**. Scrolling down, you'll find two more fields: **IO** and **Components**. The field **IO** represents the type of actions you will allow to be performed on this property. This property can be readable (`r`), writable (`w`), or subscribable (`s`). Allow all by typing `rws`. The property `components` is a components array referring to the components that you want to have on this property. Insert `["door-lock"]` to associate this property with our door-lock component.

If you click on the **JSON** button in front of the **Profile Spec** section, you should see the following profile object:

```
{
  "components": [
    {
      "id": "door-lock",
      "label": "Building Lock",
      "classes": ""
    }
  ],
  "properties": [
    {
      "id": "lock-status",
      "label": "Lock Status",
      "classes": "",
      "schema": "",
      "schemaExtension": "",
      "isTriggerable": false,
      "isActionable": false,
      "controlInterfaces": [],
      "triggers": [],
      "actions": [],
      "io": "rws",
      "onChange": false,
      "rateLimit": 0,
      "components": "[\"door-lock\"]"
    }
  ]
}
```

Save the profile, and let's start building the Galileo bridge.

Developing the Galileo bridge

Open the Intel XDK IoT Edition. Navigate to **Projects** | **Start a new project** and then select **Templates** | **Blank template** under the **INTERNET OF THINGS EMBEDDED APPLICATION** tab to create a new blank project.

To help you connect to Muzzley, let's use the `muzzley-bridge-node` library (`https://github.com/v0od0oChild/muzzley-bridge-node`). Although not an official library, it packs most of the Muzzley device-to-cloud features together and will help you with connecting and exchanging messages. Open the `package.json` file and add the line `"muzzley-bridge-node": "latest"` inside the dependencies key to allow this library to be installed in Galileo when you press the editor build button.

Create a new file and name it `config.js`. In this file, we will add all the keys and IDs we'll need to use. Copy and paste the following structure into the new `config` file:

```
var config = {};
config.account = {
  profileId: '',
  serialNumber: 'galileo-bridge-12345',
  appToken: ''
}

config.bridgeComponents = [
  {
    id: 'lock-1',
    type: 'door-lock',
    label: 'Building door lock1'
  }
];
module.exports = config;
```

Open the **App Details** lock in the Muzzley website, and there you'll find the `profileId` and `appToken` displayed. Use them to fill in the `config.account` data with your own keys. The `serialNumber` field is a unique ID that you'll need to set in order to identify this Galileo bridge.

To help us with the Galileo pin operations, we're creating the `lock.js` file, where we'll have all the pin manipulation logic. Create the file and copy the following code:

```
var mraa = require('mraa');

exports = module.exports = {};
var processingRequest = false;
```

```
var processTimer;

var pin = new mraa.Gpio(13);
pin.dir(mraa.DIR_OUT);

// Unlock the door
exports.unlockDoor = function () {
  if (processingRequest === true) return;
  processingRequest = true;
  pin.write(1);
  processTimer = setTimeout(stopUnlockingDoor, 4000);
};

// Stop unlocking the door
exports.stopUnlockingDoor = function () {
  clearTimeout(processTimer);
  pin.write(0);
  var processingRequest = false;
};
```

Since the relay will keep opening the door when active, here we'll have two main methods: unlockDoor and stopUnlockingDoor. The first method will order Galileo to set pin 13 to HIGH, which will activate the relay, close the door-unlocking circuit, and unlock the door. For security reasons, we are adding two control variables — proccessingRequest and processTimer. The processingRequest variable will ensure that only one user at a time will be able unlock the door and the processTimer will ensure that after 4 seconds, the door-unlocking system will stop whether there is Internet access or not. When a user unlocks the door, other unlocking requests for the same lock will be discarded. If the stopUnlockingDoor method is called, the timer will be cleared and the Galileo will be available for more unlock door requests.

Now, let's create our integration skeleton by pasting the following code into the main.js file:

```
// Dependencies
var muzzleyBridge = require('muzzley-bridge-node');
var lock = require('./lock');
var config = require('./config');

// Connect and subscribe to the configured Muzzley channel
muzzleyBridge.connect(config.account, config.bridgeComponents,
function (err, channel) {
  console.log('Device connected to Muzzley');

  // When a request to read the lock status arrives
```

```
channel.on('readRequest', function (user, message, callback) {
  console.log(message);
});

// When a request to change the lock status arrives
channel.on('writeRequest', function (user, message) {
  console.log(message);

  if (message.property === 'status' && message.value === true) {
  }
  if (message.property === 'status' && message.value === false) {
lock.stopUnlockingDoor();
  }
});
});
```

On connecting to Muzzley, we will receive a communication channel. We can publish and read from the subscribed component properties. We are able to publish the lock changes or perform some local actions when we receive a request.

Requests can be of two types: read or write. A read request indicates that a person allowed to be subscribed to this channel, most likely a mobile device, is requiring to obtain the value of a specific component property. In this situation, it would refer to the lock-status of the door-lock.

When receiving a write request, we will receive a command that is trying to change the value of a specific property and, in this scenario, the value of the lock-status property. This write requests will be responsible for changing the door lock status by manipulating the Galileo pins.

Build your project, upload it to Galileo, and run it using the Intel XDK. Uploading the project using this IDE will make the app to run persistently. Even when the board is rebooted, the app will restart automatically.

Developing the app interface

Heading back to the Muzzley web page, we'll now create the interface that will control the door unlocking system. In the top menu, you'll find the option **Widgets**; click on it and select **Create Widget**. Name your interface and click on **Submit**. From the widget selection menu, select the one you just created, tick the **Is interface** checkbox, and save it. Select the same widget once again, and in the left menu, you'll find the option **Editor**. Click on it to be able to edit and develop your custom interface. You'll find three text inputs, one for **HTML**, one for **CSS**, and the other one for **JavaScript**.

Starting with the HTML, let's create a main container with a button on it by copying the following lines into the HTML editor:

```
<div class="container">
  <div id="open-button"><span>UnLock</span></div>
</div>
```

Now let's take care of the styling. We'll make the displayed text not selectable using the option `user-select`. We'll add a background-color property to the main container and add some styling for the button press and release custom classes, making the button change color on press and on release. Copy and paste the stylesheet below into the CSS editor:

```
body {
  height: 100%; width: 100%; margin: 0; padding: 0;
  font-family: 'Open Sans', sans-serif;
  background-color: #fff;
}

* {
  box-sizing: border-box;
  -webkit-box-sizing: border-box;
  -moz-box-sizing: border-box;
  -webkit-tap-highlight-color: rgba(0, 0, 0, 0);
  -webkit-touch-callout: none;
  -webkit-user-select: none;
  -khtml-user-select: none;
  -moz-user-select: none;
  -ms-user-select: none;
  -ms-touch-action: none;
  user-select: none;
  -webkit-tap-hightlight-color: transparent;
}

.container{
  width: 100%;
  height: 100%;
  background-color: #efefef;
  display: table;
}

#open-button {
  width: 100px;
  height: 100px;
  border: 2px solid black;
```

```css
    margin-top: 50%;
    border-radius: 100%;
    display:table;
    margin: 0 auto 0 auto;
    background-color: #27ae60;
}

#open-button span{
    display: table-cell;
    vertical-align:middle;
    margin: 0 auto;
    width: 100%;
    text-align: center;
}

#open-button.down{
  background-color: #fec504;
  -moz-transition: all .5s ease-out;
  -webkit-transition: all .5s ease-in;
  -o-transition: all .5s ease-in;
  transition: all .5s ease-in;
}
#open-button.up{
  background-color: #27ae60;
   moz-transition: all .5s ease-out;
  -webkit-transition: all .5s ease-in;
  -o-transition: all .5s ease-in;
  transition: all .5s ease-in;
}
```

To add all the actions to our interface, we'll need to use a bit of JavaScript. We'll be using it to identify and process the browser touch events, communicate with Muzzley, set the interface size to full screen, and set the button classes to make it change its colors. To identify the `press` and `release` events, we'll need to test the events against our browser since each browser has its own event.

The Muzzley client will be running in the interface. When the event `muzzley.ready` fires, we'll subscribe the interface to the Muzzley channel. As soon as we are subscribed, we can start sending and receiving messages.

> If you want to read more about the Muzzley JS library, visit
> https://github.com/muzzley/muzzley-client.

Copy the code below to the JavaScript editor:

```javascript
var channel, EVENT_START, EVENT_RELEASE;

// Find the touch events for this browser
if('ontouchstart' in window) {
  EVENT_START = 'touchstart';
  EVENT_RELEASE = 'touchend';
} else if (window.navigator.pointerEnabled) {
  EVENT_START = 'pointerdown';
  EVENT_RELEASE = 'pointerup';
} else if (window.navigator.msPointerEnabled) {
  EVENT_START = 'MSPointerDown';
  EVENT_RELEASE = 'MSPointerUp';
} else {
  EVENT_START = 'mousedown';
  EVENT_RELEASE = 'mouseup';
}

// When Muzzley loads
muzzley.ready(function (options) {
  if(!options || !options.channels) {
    return alert('There is no channels data');
  }

  // Obtain the channel information
  // Indexing to 0 since there's only one channel (One Galileo running
this profile)
  channel = options.channels[0];

  // Subscribe to the channel
  var subscription = muzzley.subscribe( {
      namespace: 'iot',
      payload: {
        profile: channel.profileId,
        channel: channel.remoteId
      }
    });
});

// When document finishes loading, set interface to full height
$(document).ready(function() {
```

```
    $('body').css('height', window.innerHeight+'px');
    var margin = (window.innerHeight*.5) -
                         ($('#open-button').height()*.5);
    $('#open-button').css('margin-top', margin+'px');
});


// Publish a Muzzley write request to set the lock-status property
function writeLockStatus(lockStatus) {
    var data = {
            namespace: 'iot',
            payload: {
                io: 'w',
                profile: channel.profileId,
                channel: channel.remoteId,
                property: channel.id,
                component: channel.components[0],
                data: {value: lockStatus}
            }
        };
    muzzley.publish(data);
}


    // On touch, add the button class responsible to change the button
color
    // and publish Muzzley request
    $('#open-button').on(EVENT_START, function(){
      $('#open-button').removeClass();
      $('#open-button').addClass('down');
      writeLockStatus(true);
});

// On touch stop change color back and publish Muzzley request
$('#open-button').on(EVENT_RELEASE, function() {
      $('#open-button').removeClass();
      $('#open-button').addClass('up');
      writeLockStatus(false);
});
```

Save the interface changes and click on the **Apps** option in the site's top menu. Edit the app you created before, and in the **Interface UUID** option, select the interface you just created. This app is private and in order to use it, you'll need to add the user e-mails you want in the app's **Email Access list** option, separating multiple entries with commas.

> Beware that the added e-mail addresses must be the ones that will be used in the Muzzley mobile app. So, if you're logging in as a Facebook user, you'll need to add that account e-mail address.

Now you'll be able to give the app a test drive. Install the Muzzley app in your mobile device and log in. Clicking on the app's **+** button will list all the public profiles and your private ones. Locate the profile you created in the beginning of this chapter and click on it. You'll be asked for the device's serial number. Insert the `serialNumber` you defined before in the device `config` file.

After adding the channel, you'll find it listed under the **default** category. Click on it and then try pressing the interface button to unlock the door. To do this, you must have Internet access (you can use mobile Internet, such as 3G).

Check the onboard LED while you unlock the door from the app. The onboard LED should light up every time you unlock the door from the Muzzley app.

Lighting up the entrance door

Now that we can unlock our door from anywhere using the mobile phone with an Internet connection, a nice thing to have is the entrance lights turn on when you open the building door using your Muzzley app.

To do this, you can use the Muzzley workers to define rules to perform an action when the door is unlocked using the mobile app. To do this, you'll need to own one of the Muzzley-enabled smart bulbs such as Philips Hue, WeMo LED Lighting, Milight, Easybulb, or LIFX. You can find all the enabled devices in the app profiles selection list:

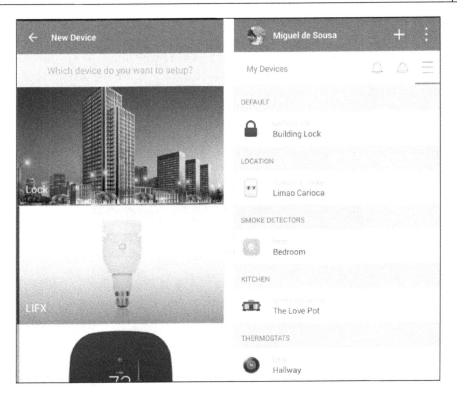

If you don't have those specific lighting devices but have another type of connected device, search the available list to see whether it is supported. If it is, you can use that instead.

Add your bulb channel to your account. You should now find it listed in your channels under the category **Lighting**. If you click on it, you'll be able to control the lights.

To activate the trigger option in the lock profile we created previously, go to the Muzzley website and head back to the **Profile Spec** app, located inside **App Details**. Expand the property lock status by clicking on the arrow sign in the **property #1 - Lock Status** section and then expand the **controlInterfaces** section. Create a new control interface by clicking on the **+controlInterface** button. In the new **controlInterface #1** section, we'll need to define the possible choices of label-values for this property when setting a rule. Feel free to insert an **id**, and in the **control interface** option, select the text-picker option. In the **config** field, we'll need to specify each of the available options, setting the display label and the real value that will be published. Insert the following JSON object:

```
{"options":[{"value":"true","label":"Lock"},
  {"value":"false","label":"Unlock"}]}.
```

Now we need to create a trigger. In the profile spec, expand the **trigger** section. Create a new trigger by clicking on the **+trigger** button. Inside the newly created section, select the `equals` condition. Create an input by clicking on **+input**, insert the ID value, insert the ID of the control interface you have just created in the **controlInterfaceId** text field. Finally, add the `[{"source":"selection.value","target":"data.value"}]`.path to map the data.

Open your mobile app and click on the workers icon. Clicking on **Create Worker** will display the worker creation menu to you. Here, you'll be able to select a channel component property as a trigger to some other channel component property:

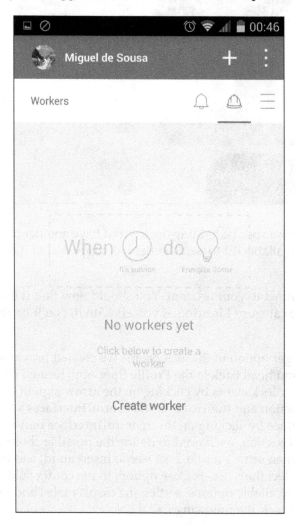

Select the lock and select the **Lock Status is equal to Unlock** trigger. Save it and select the action button. In here, select the smart bulb you own and select the **Status On** option:

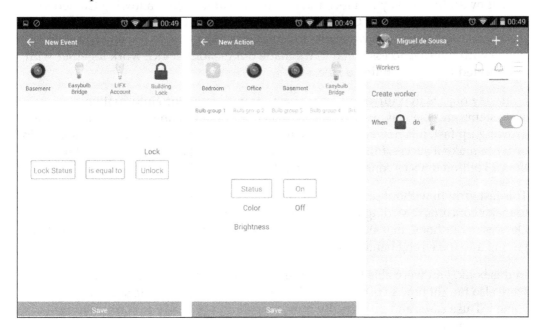

After saving this rule, give it a try and use your mobile phone to unlock the door. The smart bulb should then turn on. With this, you can configure many things in your home even before you arrive there. In this specific scenario, we used our door locker as a trigger to accomplish an action on a lightbulb. If you want, you can do the opposite and open the door when a lightbulb lights up a specific color for instance. To do it, similar to how you configured your device trigger, you just have to set up the action options in your device profile page.

Summary

In this chapter, we performed an integration with the Muzzley IoT ecosystem. We started by adding a relay to a lock inter-communicator circuit, allowing Galileo to control the circuit. We used Galileo as a bridge to connect to a local door circuit and the Muzzley platform. We were able to remotely unlock the door using a mobile phone with Internet access. Finally, we made our custom device work together with a connected bulb by defining a rule.

Everyday objects that surround us are being transformed into information ecosystems and the way we interact with them is slowly changing. Although IoT is growing up fast, it is nowadays in an early stage, and many issues must be solved in order to make it successfully scalable. By 2020, it is estimated that there will be more than 25 billion devices connected to the Internet.

This fast growth without security regulations and deep security studies are leading to major concerns regarding the two biggest IoT challenges—security and privacy. Devices in our home that are remotely controllable or even personal data information getting into the wrong hands could be the recipe for a disaster.

In this book, you were able to learn about the basics of IoT and its concepts. You were also taught how to use some of the best available tools while showing you some IoT use cases and projects. By now, you should be ready to start creating your own projects.

Index

Thank you for buying
Internet of Things with Intel Galileo

About Packt Publishing

Packt, pronounced 'packed', published its first book, *Mastering phpMyAdmin for Effective MySQL Management*, in April 2004, and subsequently continued to specialize in publishing highly focused books on specific technologies and solutions.

Our books and publications share the experiences of your fellow IT professionals in adapting and customizing today's systems, applications, and frameworks. Our solution-based books give you the knowledge and power to customize the software and technologies you're using to get the job done. Packt books are more specific and less general than the IT books you have seen in the past. Our unique business model allows us to bring you more focused information, giving you more of what you need to know, and less of what you don't.

Packt is a modern yet unique publishing company that focuses on producing quality, cutting-edge books for communities of developers, administrators, and newbies alike. For more information, please visit our website at www.packtpub.com.

About Packt Open Source

In 2010, Packt launched two new brands, Packt Open Source and Packt Enterprise, in order to continue its focus on specialization. This book is part of the Packt Open Source brand, home to books published on software built around open source licenses, and offering information to anybody from advanced developers to budding web designers. The Open Source brand also runs Packt's Open Source Royalty Scheme, by which Packt gives a royalty to each open source project about whose software a book is sold.

Writing for Packt

We welcome all inquiries from people who are interested in authoring. Book proposals should be sent to author@packtpub.com. If your book idea is still at an early stage and you would like to discuss it first before writing a formal book proposal, then please contact us; one of our commissioning editors will get in touch with you.

We're not just looking for published authors; if you have strong technical skills but no writing experience, our experienced editors can help you develop a writing career, or simply get some additional reward for your expertise.

Internet of Things with the Arduino Yún

ISBN: 978-1-78328-800-7   Paperback: 112 pages

Projects to help you build a world of smarter things

1. Learn how to interface various sensors and actuators to the Arduino Yún and send this data in the cloud.

2. Explore the possibilities offered by the Internet of Things by using the Arduino Yún to upload measurements to Google Docs, upload pictures to Dropbox, and send live video streams to YouTube.

3. Learn how to use the Arduino Yún as the brain of a robot that can be completely controlled via Wi-Fi.

Cloning Internet Applications with Ruby

ISBN: 978-1-84951-106-3   Paperback: 336 pages

Make your own TinyURL, Twitter, Flickr, or Facebook using Ruby

1. Build your own custom social networking, URL shortening, and photo sharing websites using Ruby.

2. Deploy and launch your custom high-end web applications.

3. Learn what makes popular social networking sites such as Twitter and Facebook tick.

Building a Rich Internet Application with Vaadin [Video]

ISBN: 978-1-78328-892-2   Duration: 02:19 hours

Easily create powerful, modern web apps with this rich Java framework

1. An iterative approach to building Vaadin applications, taking you from first steps to a complete app.

2. Use navigation and CSS to create a complete web application.

3. Learn how to develop custom widgets and components with Vaadin.

ExtGWT Rich Internet Application Cookbook

ISBN: 978-1-84951-518-4   Paperback: 366 pages

80 recipes to build rich Java web apps on the robust GWT platform, with Sencha ExtGWT

1. Take your ExtGWT web development skills to the next level.

2. Create stunning UIs with several layouts and templates in a fast and simple manner.

3. Enriched with code and screenshots for easy and quick grasp.

Please check **www.PacktPub.com** for information on our titles